Shabbat is a very special festival. We celebrate Shabbat every Friday night and Saturday. We light candles and share a special bread called challah bread.

Shabbat is a time of rest. We rest because we remember the story of how God created the world.

On the first day there was nothing, no light, no animals, no people – nothing!

So God said, "Let there be light," and it happened.

God was pleased and said, "Aahh that is good!"

On the second day God filled the earth with water. There were flowing rivers, streams and, of course, the sea.

God was pleased and said, "Aahh that is good!"

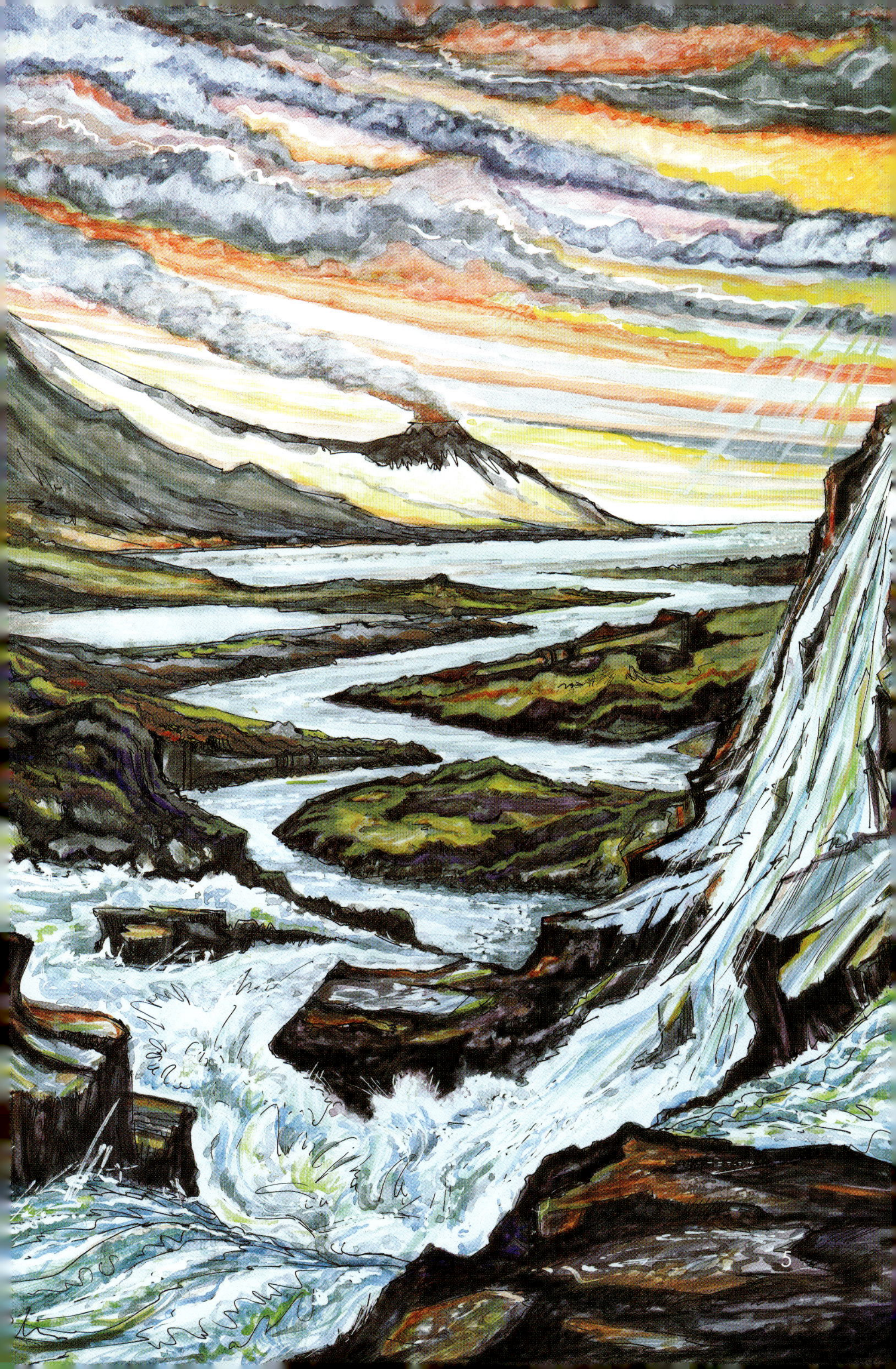

Then God looked at the earth.
"It needs some plants, trees and flowers," he thought.

So that is what he made. All sorts of different ones.

Tall ones.
Short ones.
Fat ones.
Thin ones.
Plain flowers.
Spotty flowers.
Stripy flowers.

And for every one he said,
"Aahh that is good!"

This was the third day.

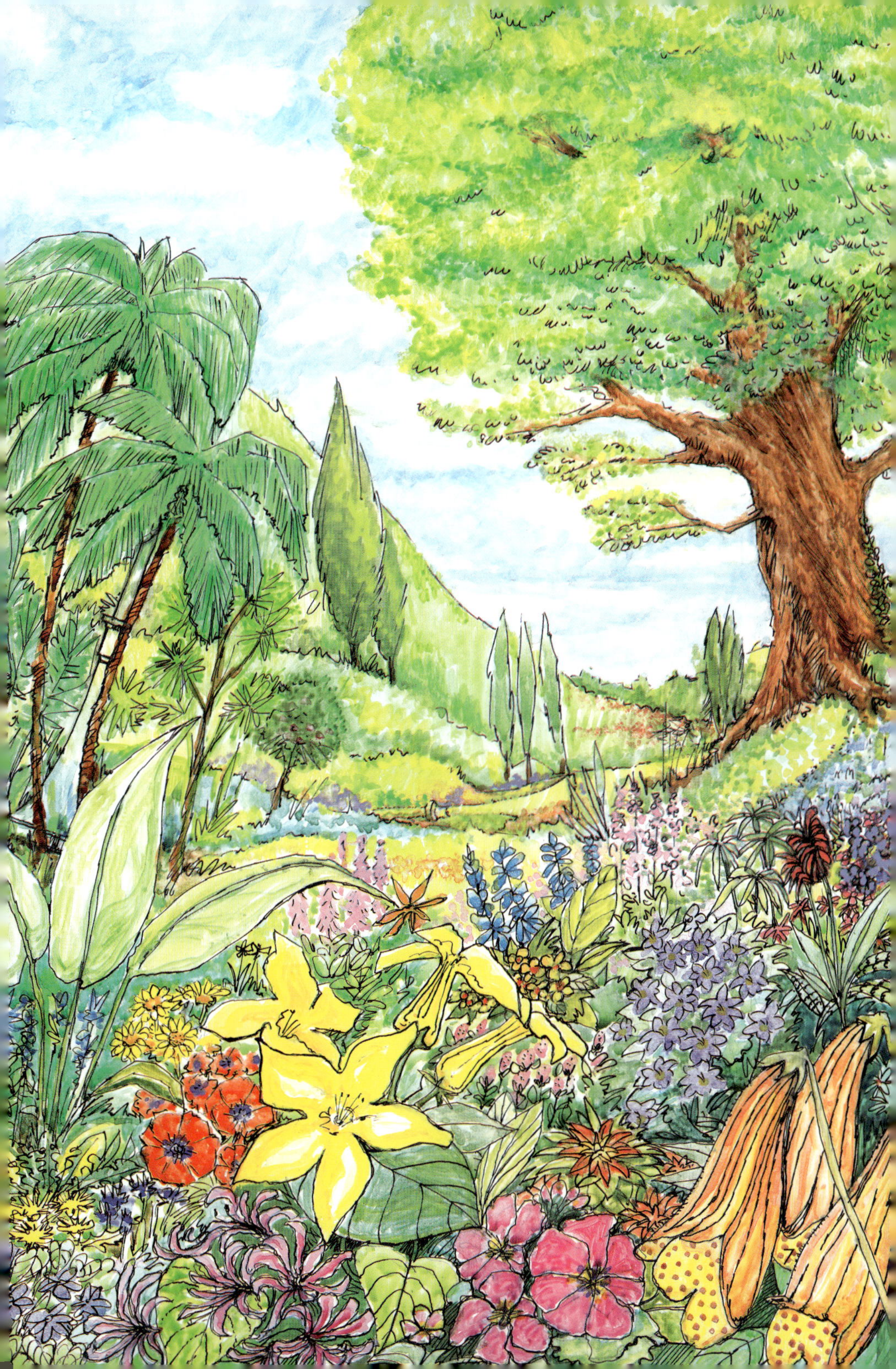

Then God decided to make day and night.

The day was to be sunny and bright.

The night was to be darker, but not dark because there were millions of stars to light the sky. This was to help us remember the different seasons and festivals through the year.

And God said, "Aahh that is good!"

This was the fourth day.

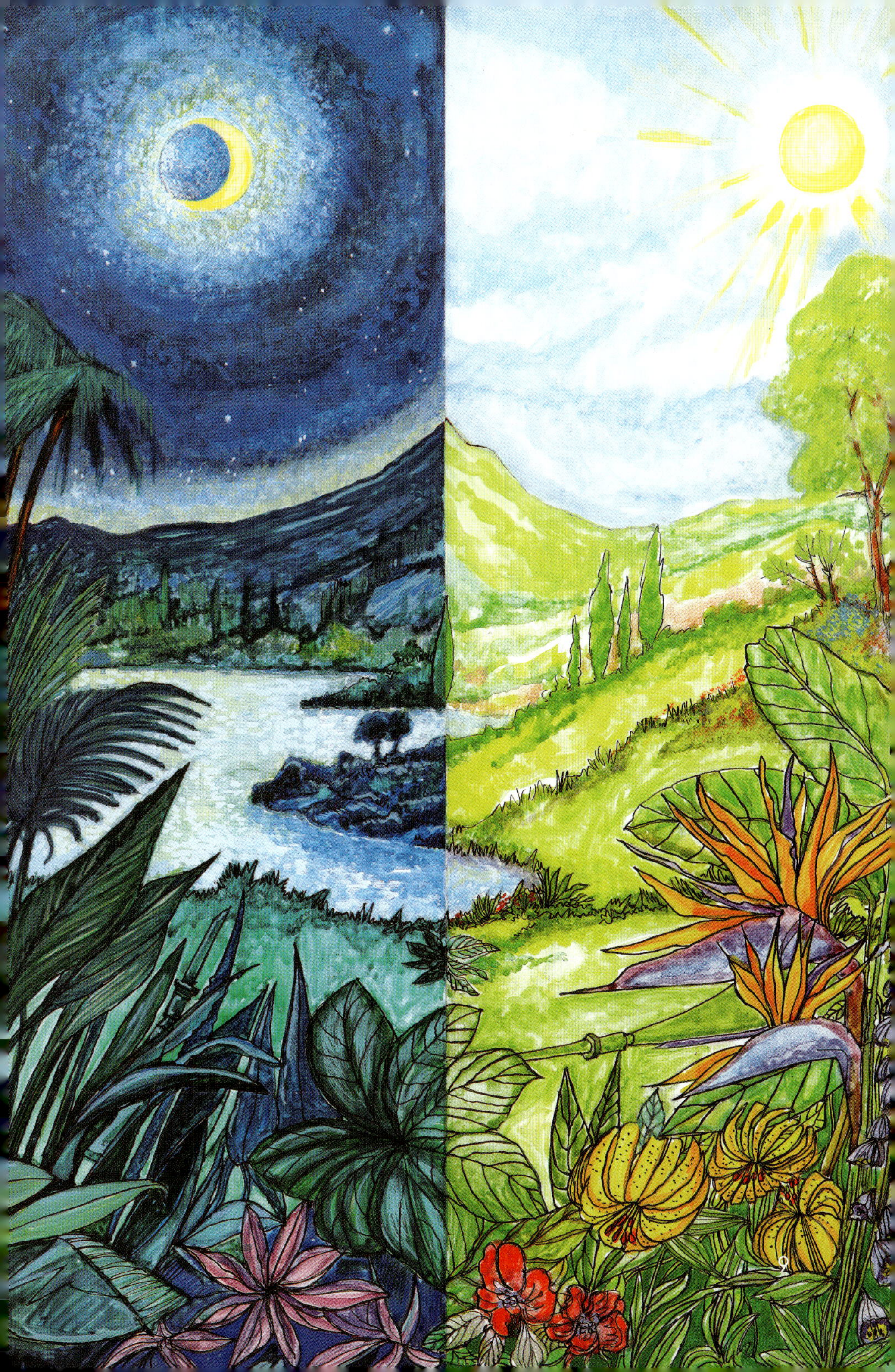

Then God made fish and birds and blessed them, saying, "Grow and multiply."
That was on the fifth day.

And he looked at them and said,
"Aahh that is good!"

On the sixth day he made lots of different creatures. There were cows and horses, snakes and elephants and lots of other animals.

How many of them can you list?

And God looked at them all and said,
"Aahh that is good!"

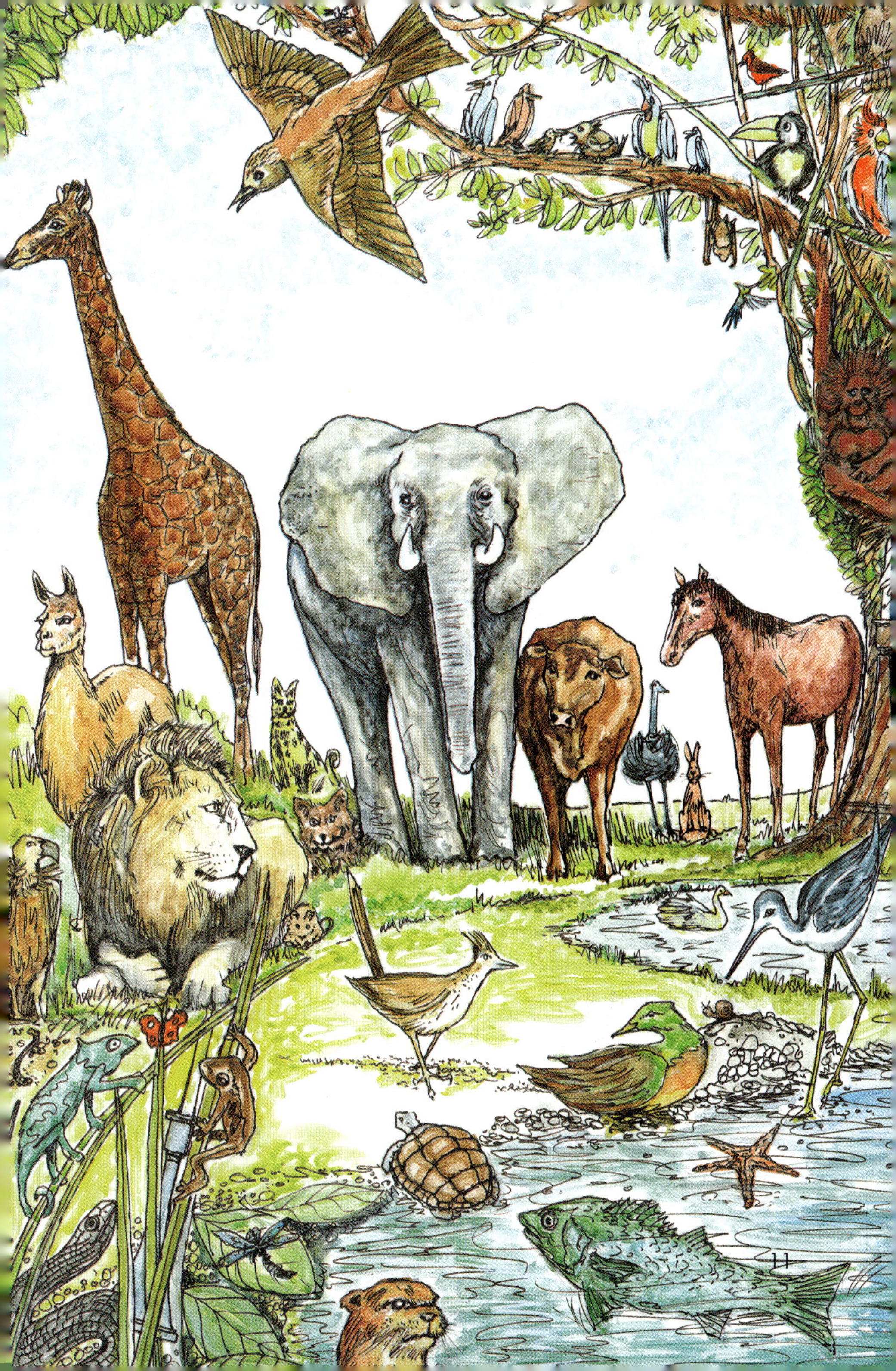

Then last of all God made people, a man and a woman. He called the man Adam, and the woman Eve. He told them to look after the earth and care for all he had created. This was on the sixth day.

By the time the seventh day came, God was so pleased with his work that he made the day special. It is called Shabbat, the Sabbath.

In the story all people are descendants of Adam and Eve, so we all have to look after God's world!

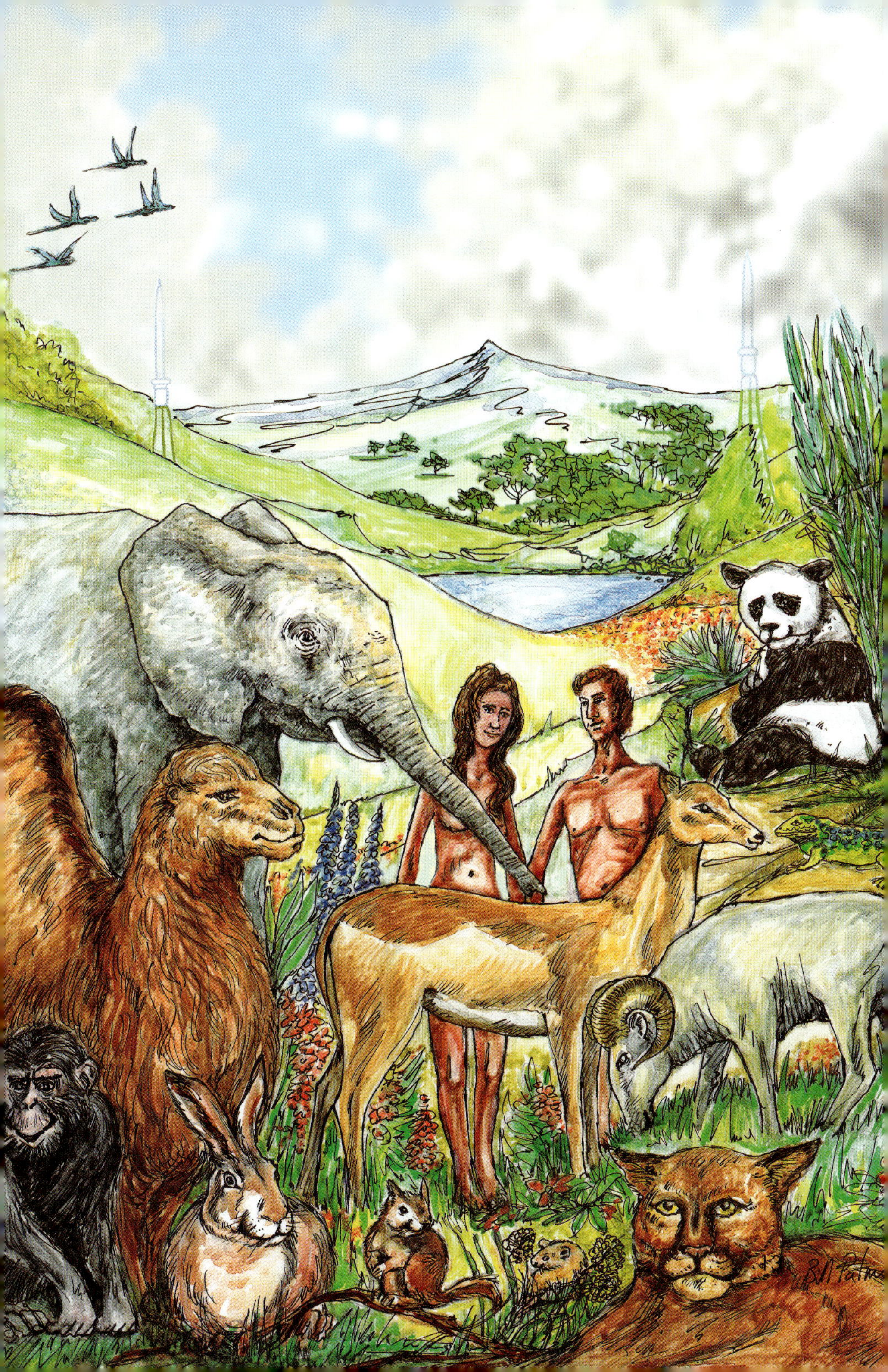

That is why we light our special candles and eat our special bread. Because we believe God made everything, for one day a week we stop and say thank you to God with a special prayer:

"Blessed are You, Lord our God, King of the Universe, who has made us holy and commanded us to light the Shabbat candles."

And I say, "Aahh that is good!"

15

Can you tell a story about Shabbat?

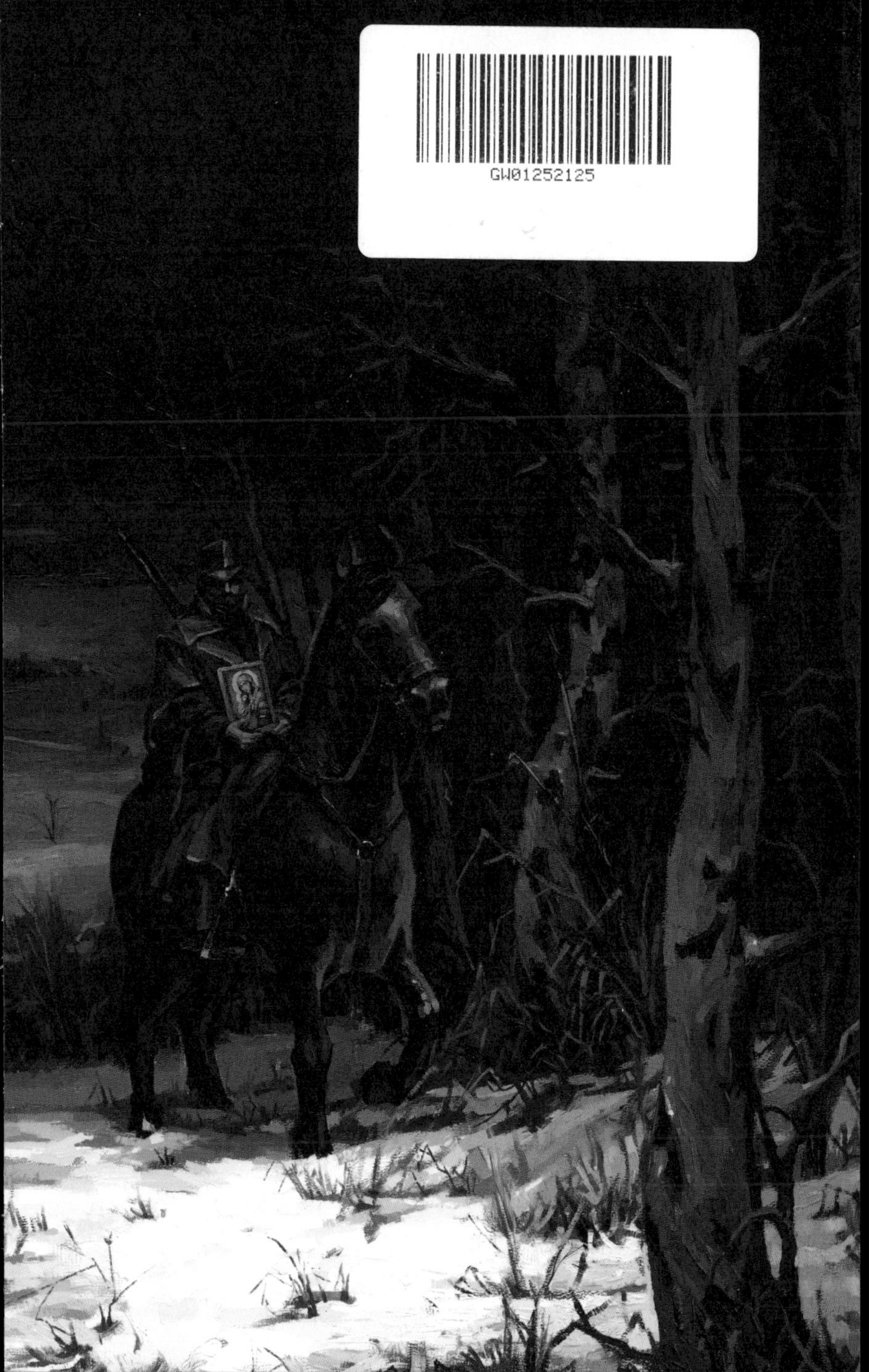

Mauser, Max. *The Ghosts of Olesko*.
Original title: *Rittet fra Olesko* (1935)
©FREKK 2025
https://frekk.eu/
Translated by: Oda Rygh and Arlen Jamie
DESIGN: Frekk
PRINT: Baltoprint
ISBN: 978–82–93097–75–4

THE GHOSTS OF OLESKO

Max Mauser

ALSO IN THE NORDIC CRIME LIBRARY

The Hall of Mirrors - Stein Riverton

The Iron Chariot - Stein Riverton

SITTING ON TOP OF A VOLCANO

At the start of *The Ghosts of Olesko*, the main characters live in a somewhat boring place just outside Oslo. Nothing happens, complains the book's heroine, Anne Marie, but her companions Adrian Krebs and Waldemar Wiig are content. On the continent, ill winds are blowing, and old disputes must be settled. To resolve something from the past, Krebs asks Wiig to visit Germany to do him a favour.

Before long, the ghosts of the Great War come tumbling into Norway, a country that was neutral during the conflict, and with them, they bring bad omens for the future.

Both the author, Jonas Lie (1899–1945), using the pseudonym Max Mauser, and the characters in *The Ghosts of Olesko* are, to use a picture from Berlin's roaring 20s, living on top of a volcano. They know it is bubbling beneath them, but not that it will erupt. In hindsight, it is obvious what is coming.

Jonas Lie grew up in one of Norway's most important cultural circles. He was the grandson of the famous Norwegian author Jonas Lie (1833–1908). The elder Lie was considered one of the four great Norwegian writers with Henrik Ibsen (1828–1906), Bjønstjerne Bjørnson (1832–1910), and Alexander Kielland (1849–1906). Lie was also a cousin of the Norwegian architect Helge Thiis (1897–1972), and his uncle by marriage was one of Norway's most renowned art historians, Jens Thiis (1870–1942).

His cultural upbringing is evident in *Ghosts of Olesko*. It is an upper middle class setting where Wiig takes pleasure in knowing all about how to wine and dine his guests. Krebs is a musician, and we quickly get introduced to an art historian. A key part of the plot revolves around the power a work of art can have on people. Had the main characters not encountered an amazing icon at a certain point, no 'crime' would have been committed. We get historical analyses of works of art, and learn about people who lost their mind after seeing Nefertiti's bust in Berlin.

Lie, however, did not pursue a cultural career. He earned a law degree and opened his law practice in 1925. In 1930, he became a police superintendent at the Bergen Police Department and, in 1931, a superintendent at the newly established State Police in Oslo, the Norwegian Special Forces Branch, where he was promoted to deputy chief the following year.

At the same time, he made an international career, trying to resolve problems inherited from the past. In the winter of 1934/1935, he served as an international police officer in Saarland. The Saar had been separated from Germany after the Great War and administered by the League of Nations. France had been given control of the Saar's coal mines, but at Versailles it had been agreed that after fifteen years of League of Nations administration, the population should be able to decide whether Saar should return to Germany, or become a part of France. Lie was one of the monitors.

Three years later, he again joined the League of Nations delegation to try to solve the Hatay dispute, and organise a referendum to determine if the province of Alexandrette should belong to Turkey or Syria.

His most spectacular assignment as a police officer came when the communist leader Leon Trotsky, who had been in exile in Norway since 1935, was expelled in 1936. Trotsky was granted asylum in Mexico – and Lie was given the task of accompanying him there, a noted anti–communist protecting a communist leader.

(Interestingly though, Lie had not received the assignment when writing *The Ghosts of Olesko;* Trotsky, as the head of the Red Army at the end of the First World War, plays an indirect role in the novel. Lie describes the Red Army's rampage in Ukraine in detail). From Mexico, Lie travelled to the United States, where he sought out John Edgar Hoover and was allowed to study the FBI's working methods.

In the midst of all this, he wrote five crime novels, which were published under the pseudonym Max Mauser from 1932 to 1939. *The Diamond of Death* (1932) (Dødsdiamanten) was followed by *The Devil's Birthday* (1934) (Natten til Fandens geburtsdag), *The Ghosts of Olesko* (1935) (Rittet fra Olesko), and *Fetish* (1937) (Fetisj). They were all sensational successes in the Nordics. His crime writing career ended with *A Shark Follows the Boat* (En hai følger båten, 1938), inspired by his trip with Trotsky to Mexico and his visit to the FBI.

Today, it is hard not to be fascinated by the fact that these crime novels were written by an author who, at the time of their writing, held a leading position in the police.

They are action–packed books, but the dark undercurrents that later will be the hallmark of Nordic crime literature are clearly present. Mauser is not copying his contemporary British writers; he is mixing his own brew. In *The Ghosts of Olesko,* the male characters are brooding, torn by the past, or mentally corrupted. They all have somewhat disturbing personalities. Apart from the detectives, the most stable character is Anne Marie, and she feels limited by not being a man.

The Ghosts of Olesko was probably written during Lie's spare moments as an international policeman in Saar. Working there he would be painfully aware of the legacy of the First World War, even though Saar was at the western border.

In the book, one of the soldiers travel across war–torn Ukraine. Not all of them make it home. One joins the Ukrainian Independence Army, while another is forced to join the Red Army. Later they frequently point out that Norwegians, living in peace since the Napoleonic Wars, could not comprehend what has happened on the continent – what suffering people have endured, and how borders changed. For them, it was just a newspaper article.

In 1939, the volcano erupted – and Lie wrote no more crime novels. Late that autumn, he was ordered to Finnmark to ensure the Soviet–Finnish Winter War did not spill over into Norway. He quickly became head of the surveillance police in Kirkenes, with leadership of the surveillance service in Eastern Finnmark which borders Russia and Finland.

Then on 9 of April 1940, Germany invaded Norway. Vidkun Quisling appointed Lie as a minister in his coup government. Lie, who was still in Finnmark, flatly rejected the offer and chose to fight with the Norwegian forces. But although he rejected Quisling, there was no doubt about his pro–German sympathies. In the summer of 1940, Reichskommissar Josef Terboven wanted to replace Quisling with Lie. Instead, on 30 May, at the request of the Germans, Lie was appointed police inspector and liaison officer between the Norwegian and German police.

At that point, Lie's private volcano erupted, and to a certain extent, this was the case for a sizable part of the Norwegian cultural elite. Readers will notice that the Norwegians in the book were fluent in German, and pre–war German was the Norwegians' second language. He was not the only one from his cultural background whose values proved to be totally wrong when the Second World War started. It split families.

In the Bjørnson family, several children were positive about Nazism, but the youngest son Erling turned his father's house into a propaganda centre for national socialism. At the same time, his oldest son Bjørn Bjørnson, who was the director of the Norwegian National Theatre, became an ardent opponent of national socialism.

Norway's most famous author and Nobel Prize winner Knut Hamsun (1859–1952) was an enthusiastic national socialist, and the most famous living composer Christian Sinding (1856–1941) was also branded a Nazi after the war.

Professor of Literature Willy Dahl suggests that the author and his pen name alter ego had different personalities; Mauser was more of a classical conservative than Lie. He was at least critical of Nazi Germany. In Olesko, Wiig hesitates before going to Germany:

But reports from acquaintances and friends who had made such trips held me back.

'You'll be disappointed,' they had said, 'times have changed; travel isn't what it used to be.'

I didn't care to sit around waiting for some official to confiscate my newspapers because they were banned, or for a customs officer to search my wallet. I'd rather stay home and travel in my thoughts.

The writer Mauser also often shows mercy where the police officer Lie would not.

When the National Unity Party (Nasjonal Samling) was declared the only legal party on 25 September 1940, Lie changed his view of Quisling and the NS. He joined the party and was appointed Minister of Police in the provisional government.

In 1945, Jonas Lie died under uncertain circumstances in a bunker outside Oslo. He was one of the most hated men in the country. In that bunker one of Norway's best crime writers also died.

'We often think anyone who writes good books must be a good person. Jonas Lie, the person behind the pseudonym Max Mauser, was not. In his final years, it was the brutal devil in him that took over.'

Willy Melkior Dahl, 'Max Mauser – but Jonas Lie. A study in poetry and life' (1990), is a Norwegian professor emeritus of Nordic literature.

Nicolai Strøm–Olsen, publisher, Frekk

Note from the publisher:
This book reflects the prevailing attitudes at the time of writing, which some readers might find offensive. We as publishers do not condone these attitudes, but recognise that this history cannot be erased.

CHAPTER I

'Every day the world is spurred into action,' said Anne Marie feverishly, tipping a log with her foot so that it fell into the firewood basket with a crash.

She crumpled up her newspaper, threw it into the fireplace, and continued loudly and harshly: 'Here it's all about men, men everywhere; tough, strong–willed men who can hate, love, and kill …'

Anne Marie's hair flamed red. The newspaper caught fire instantly, burning brightly for a long second. When Anne Marie was in that mood, it was best to keep quiet and wait for it to pass.

'But we just sit up here,' she continued, her voice carrying a tone of hostility, 'we sit here on Hasselbakken, and absolutely nothing happens to us except that Adrian occasionally gets a solo on his harp or a spot on the radio. And then we're all so excited, my God, how thrilled we are! We practically revolve around the world's events!'

The fireplace crackled, and a red flame licked the sooty wall. The fire's glow spread into the dark room and lit up Anne Marie's golden hair. Against the background beams, Adrian's harp stood fully illuminated; it was as if its tense strings were trembling.

'Perhaps not everyone gets the chance,' I interjected carefully. 'What do you expect from peaceful Hasselbakken?'

'The world's on fire out there, big things are happening, and we sit here, outside and unnecessary.'

'Well, at least it's not burning here,' Adrian remarked offhandedly, and, as if changing the subject, he asked me whether I thought the house was insured enough. He even mentioned the amount. Perhaps he was trying to distract Anne Marie with something more mundane, but she immediately cut him off:

'Yes, you've insured everything. You're sitting safe on your perch, going off to your regular job without caring that men just as often create the opportunity as the opportunity creates the men. We sit here, dozing off, and you're satisfied with it. You think you've got it good —'

'I've got you,' said Adrian jokingly. 'Remember, I have you, while you only have me.'

'You lack ambition, initiative, and a sense of adventure ...'

'Your husband has proven himself,' I said diplomatically. 'He's been a soldier, fought in a war, and gone through two marriages, so it's worse for an old bachelor like me, whom fate never bothered to meet halfway.'

'But has he ever actually told you what he achieved?' Anne Marie asked. 'Has he told you anything other than that his ears froze in Galicia, that he was hungry, and that he played the trumpet in an "Imperial and Royal" military band?'

'Those who fought in the war don't like talking about it.'

I thought my arguments were solid and convincing, but Anne Marie swept them aside and turned directly to Adrian:

'Tell us!' she said. 'Tell us something for once; let's hear what you were involved in.'

Her whole frame quivered with impatience.

Anne Marie could sometimes be like that with Adrian. He was used to it and probably didn't take it more seriously than it deserved. He removed the pipe from his mouth, stared back into the fire, and replied calmly that he'd told his small story many times. He'd been with the band, not much had happened, as he said, he played the trumpet ...

'But in the end,' I said, mainly to get him talking, 'when the war ended and demobilisation came, you were deep into Russia, weren't you? You told me once. How did you manage to get back without being captured?'

Adrian brushed his forehead. I realised I was bothering him.

'We rode and rode,' he finally answered reluctantly. 'And it rained non–stop. It was late autumn 1918 …'

He fell silent.

'You might as well talk to the wall,' Anne Marie snapped irritably. 'Sometimes I feel a burning urge to shake him up. Don't think for a second he's as indifferent as he pretends. Every evening he listens to that German war comrades' broadcast; he can sit for hours as long as it's on, and he never misses it when he's home.'

'War comrades' broadcast,' I said, 'what a mouthful. What is it?'

'The idea is that old war buddies who've lost contact can try to reconnect,' Adrian answered. 'It often works, and it's fun to listen to. It has little to do with the war, really; that's not why I tune in.'

'Didn't you have any comrades you cared about?' asked Anne Marie.

'You know I was Austrian back then,' Adrian replied evasively, 'and against all rules, I served my final year with a Rhineland division. My comrades were strangers to me, and as an artist I had little in common with them.'

'He's a wall,' said Anne Marie bitterly, turning to me, 'a big, stubborn stone wall. But now I'm going to play something and shake him up.'

Adrian said nothing but tossed another log into the fire, and a burst of crackling sparks flew upwards. Behind us, a colder light switched on; Anne Marie had taken her seat at the piano and was shuffling her sheet music. She tested a few notes, then suddenly and unexpectedly a staccato chord leapt into the room, followed by a cheerful fanfare that bubbled from the keys, and we heard Anne Marie's bright voice in a devil–may–care teasing refrain:

'Uns ist alles einerlei, einerlei – einerlei …'
Between the runs came quick, merry notes, then the refrain again, over and over …
'uns ist alles einerlei, einerlei, einerlei …'
Again and again.
'Stop,' begged Adrian. 'For God's sake, stop!'
Anne Marie abruptly stopped playing and returned to her armchair.
'Alright,' she said, 'but only if you tell us something.'
I stepped in and tried to change the subject, mentioning that I'd been thinking of travelling to Germany for the holidays. I wanted to see Rothenburg and southern Germany, and asked Adrian if he thought travel money and such would be difficult. In short, I'd lived in one place for too long, five years just outside Oslo; it was enough. I was starting to grow roots and become a local …

Another half hour passed chatting by the fire; another evening was over. Outside it was dusk; the air was damp and chilly, but already held a hint of spring. The road down the hill was muddy.

I stopped instinctively when I heard the veranda door open. For a moment, I thought I saw Anne Marie's figure in the doorway, but I realised I was mistaken and continued. Further down the hill, I heard music. Anne Marie was playing the same melody – *uns ist alles einerlei …*

But she wasn't singing anymore.

That was how my journey to Cologne began. As I sat there by the fire at Hasselbakken, on a whim, I concocted a holiday plan just to change the subject and help my friend Adrian. I hadn't seriously considered travelling abroad; I'd often thought about finally exploring the world, returning to the old places where I spent an unforgettable time as a student a small lifetime ago. But reports from friends who had made such trips held me back.

'You'll be disappointed,' they had said, 'times have changed; travel isn't what it used to be.'

I didn't care to sit around waiting for some official to confiscate my newspapers because they were banned, or for a customs officer to search my wallet. I'd rather stay home and travel in my thoughts. I was content with my circumstances: three lovely rooms with a bath and a landlady who was far too attentive, sometimes to the point of being almost annoyingly caring. Adrian even claimed I was a little afraid of her.

I liked living in the countryside. My work in Oslo mainly consisted of occasionally stopping by Wiig and Westerberg's Agricultural Machinery Company, which my uncle left me when he passed away. Fortunately, it turned out to run itself, thanks to an experienced and reliable manager. When 'the boss' — that's me – drops in now and then, I'm greeted with good–natured, joking condescension from the entire staff. I pretend not to notice, but inwardly I comfort myself with the thought that, even if I don't know much about tractors and farming machines, there are still other things of value in this world. Face to face with myself, I don't even shy away from the claim that it's perhaps just as important to understand a good red wine as a good milk separator; though, of course, in today's world, you can hardly state such heretical views.

As I said, I like living in the countryside. I enjoy a good dinner, a fine wine, and a few dear friends. And since Adrian Krebs and his wife moved out here two years ago, I had been content. We saw each other nearly every day, certainly several times a week. We came and went at each other's homes like old confidants. It had always been that way, except for three weeks last summer when they went on holiday to the west coast. We missed each other.

Two days after the evening I've just written about, Adrian came up to see me in the morning. I remember the day clearly; it was sunny, the first warm day of summer after a cold, damp, wet spring.

CHAPTER I

I noticed that Adrian seemed different than usual; nervous and restless, speaking distractedly and jumping between topics. As I opened the mineral water, I stole a sideways glance at him. His forehead was damp, and the small wet curls of dark hair clung to his temples. His fine, pale, intelligent features were tense and uneasy. For the first time, it occurred to me that somewhere among Adrian's ancestors, there might have been a trace of Jewish heritage. I also wondered what the cause of his unrest might be. Was Anne Marie still in her bad mood from the other night?

'When are you travelling?' Adrian suddenly asked.

'Travelling?'

'Yes,' he said, feigning indifference. 'Didn't you talk about going to Germany, to the Rhine and Rothenburg?'

'It was a passing idea,' I said, 'something that came to me in the moment. It takes some doing to actually get going. One day I'll manage, but when, I don't know.'

'It would do you good,' Adrian murmured.

'Of course,' I said. 'Everyone benefits from a bit of travel abroad, if only to learn to appreciate what we have at home. But, as you know, I'm a creature of habit. I don't like the idea of rushing off into the unknown on a whim. It would be different if you and your wife could come with me …'

'I can't right now,' Adrian mumbled.

'It's not urgent,' I said, offering him a cigar. 'I can plan around you both.'

'It's not just that.'

'If it's money trouble, you know I'm doing very well,' I said. 'I've got some spare cash.. You could pay me back as it suits you …'

'Thanks,' said Adrian. 'That's kind of you, but it's not exactly money I was thinking about.'

He paused a little and continued slowly, cautiously:

'The thing is, you could do me a great favour …'

'With pleasure,' I said. 'Just tell me what it is.'

'You could leave right away and sort something out for me along the way.'

It took me by surprise. I thought about it; perhaps this was exactly the push I needed to get moving. At the very least, I wasn't entirely dismissive. I told Adrian that, as I said, I hadn't planned on travelling immediately, but if it really mattered to him, I would certainly try my best.

'Yes,' said Adrian quickly; it was as if he seized the opportunity with both hands. 'Yes, you could do me a great service. You speak fluent German, don't you?'

'I studied in Bonn for three semesters.'

'It's very important to me,' Adrian continued earnestly – and it was unlike him to be so insistent – 'that you are in Cologne on the seventh of June. You can help me out, but I must ask you to forgive me for not being fully open with you. I must place a great deal of trust in your friendship here and ask you to act on my behalf without questioning the reasons behind certain things. I can't explain; it's not in my power to do so. I'm bound to secrecy. Are you still willing?'

'This sounds mysterious and odd,' I said. 'At the very least, you'll have to tell me a little more about the task. I'd rather not get involved in something without knowing the implications.'

'It's simply about attending a meeting on my behalf,' said Adrian. 'You only need to observe and listen, and tell me about it later. There's nothing illegal. You won't be drawn into anything, nor will you have to do anything at all; I give you my word of honour.'

'Very well,' I said. 'Let's have a toast, and then you can tell me more.'

'But first, you must give me your word of honour that you won't speak of this to anyone,' said Adrian earnestly after we'd toasted. 'And above all, not to Anne Marie.'

I gave him my word.

Adrian looked relieved and took another sip of his drink, even though he'd just finished one.

'I can't tell you much more than this: the meeting is connected to the past,' he continued. 'It will take place in a restaurant in Cologne on the seventh of June at four o'clock. The restaurant is called *Heilige Lampe*. You'll need to travel so you arrive in Cologne on the morning train; don't bring any luggage and don't check into a hotel. When the time comes, go to the meeting place and ask for the private room, which likely lies behind the main restaurant. There, you'll probably meet a few gentlemen, and you'll tell them you've come to attend the meeting. If they ask for your name, say you're Ekki Muller, and that you're Finnish. Under no circumstances should you say you're Norwegian. If you're turned away, hand them this written authorisation.'

He handed me a folded piece of paper. I opened it and read. The text was in German. It read: *'Herr Ekki Muller is authorised to attend on my behalf.'* It was signed: *Wolfgang Steiner*.

Adrian had clearly prepared for me to make this journey on his behalf. He'd even gone so far as to prepare a written letter of authorisation. This irked me slightly; I looked at him. 'Wolfgang Steiner?'

'It's as good a name as any,' he replied quickly and nervously. 'My own must remain out of it. The same goes for my whereabouts. That's why you must return to Berlin on the evening train the same day. And if you feel that someone is following you, trying to find out who you are or where you're going, you must, without fail, shake them off. I trust you in this, Valdemar.'

My irritation had subsided. 'It's a peculiar assignment, under any circumstances,' I said cheerfully, for the absurdity of the entire situation was beginning to dawn on me. 'Do you remember how Anne Marie recently complained that nothing ever happens? And now here you are, involving me in all this. I feel like a man set to run a sack race, only the sack is over his head.'

We mixed ourselves another drink.

'So, you are willing?' said Adrian.

'At the very least, I'm thoroughly intrigued,' I replied.

Adrian's expression darkened, and the hand holding his glass trembled.

I continued:

'But can't you tell me a little more about the people I'll be meeting down there?'

'I don't know myself,' he said in a hollow tone, staring blankly into the air. But then he pulled himself together. 'Yes, one person is likely to be present; a thin, greying gentleman of about fifty. He walks with a limp and uses a cane. His name is … no, it's best you don't know.'

'Your candour could use some improvement,' I said, slightly offended.

'It's for your own good,' Adrian replied. 'I assure you, it's best you don't know anything.'

'But what am I to say and do? How am I supposed to behave at this meeting?'

Adrian took a deep sip. It was a while before he responded.

'You are to remain completely passive,' he finally said. 'Simply state that you come on behalf of Wolfgang Steiner, who has withdrawn from the world and wishes only to live in peace. Beyond that, observe and listen, so that afterwards you can describe everything to me. That's what matters.'

We poured another drink. Suddenly Adrian changed course, saying it was all nonsense, that it didn't matter, and he asked me to draw a line under everything that had been said; there was nothing to it, really. I argued that I would gladly make the journey. In fact, it was exactly the sort of mission that appealed to me; I had developed a real curiosity about it. So we sat there, rambling on over our third drink. Adrian couldn't hold his drink in the morning; I suspected he'd catch trouble from Anne Marie later, especially since he was due to perform that evening.

After he left, I noticed he had forgotten a newspaper. It was a German one: *Völkischer Beobachter*, dated 28 May. I picked it up and began leafing through it. By chance, my eyes caught the word *Kriegskameradsendung*, and since we'd recently spoken of that, my eyes continued down the column and suddenly stopped at another familiar term: *Heilige Lampe*. My attention piqued, I read the advertisement carefully. It was indeed an advert:

'Hallo listeners of the War Comrades Broadcast —' it read, in bold type. Then followed the words: *'Olesko, 13 December 1918'*, in spaced lettering, and then, in regular print:

' … important meeting, final notice, last assembly – private room, Heilige Lampe, Cologne, 7 June, 16:00.'

I heard footsteps on the veranda steps. Adrian returned. I quickly folded the newspaper and placed it on the chair.

'I forgot something,' he said, breathless. 'I left a newspaper.'

He picked it up and stood for a moment.

'I've changed my mind,' he said suddenly, in a thick, resolute voice. 'I do want you to go, after all. If you're still willing to do me that great favour?'

We shook hands on it. Adrian repeated his instructions. We sat together for quite a while.

CHAPTER II

The restaurant *Heilige Lampe* turned out to be in central Cologne, in the shadow of the Cathedral. It was nestled deep at the base of that colossus which, from a massive, powerful foundation, sends spires like needle–pointed missiles towards a cheerful, dark–blue summer sky.

I wandered about that morning, revelling in being out in the world again, hearing a foreign language all around me. Wherever I stood or walked, I could see the church's soaring towers; now close by, now far away. But they were always there. It put me in a peculiar, expectant mood.

'*Heilige Lampe*', I thought. We were in the forecourts of Rome, in the stronghold of Catholicism. Monks walked the streets, and priests in large black hats.

I had followed Adrian's instructions precisely. I'd come directly from Berlin, my return ticket in my pocket, and I had not checked into any hotel; I was a free man, a wanderer without a fixed abode. My first task was to locate the restaurant. Once I'd done that, I felt free to enjoy myself. I roamed the city, observing the new Germany, strolling the streets, and feeling that time was truly my own.

Later that morning, I found myself in an old, unusual tavern – a *Ratsherrenkeller* with thick, cool stone walls and tiny stained–glass windows set in heavy lead frames. The waiter, dressed in a monk's robe with a rope around his waist and wooden sandals on his feet, warmly recommended a *Brauneberger Juffer*.

I was utterly captivated by all this foreignness. A quiet joy intoxicated me, and the *Brauneberger Juffer* slipped golden and sunny into my blood like the Moselle from which it came, gently blending with the Rhine on a warm summer day. The wine was divine; full–bodied, with all the mellow, tired sweetness of late summer, and soft as the smile of a Madonna.

It cast a light veil over my morning. Before I knew it, it was late, and I had to leave. I decided to take my dinner at *Heilige Lampe*, to familiarise myself with the place ahead of the meeting and to get a sense of the atmosphere. After all, it might turn out to be a shady place, and one should be prepared.

But my concern proved unnecessary. I quickly realised that the restaurant clearly belonged to the better sort; it was well–frequented, the food was excellent, and there was an air of a 'renowned kitchen' about the place. However, observing the other guests proved hopeless; if any were there for the same reason I was, it would have been impossible to tell. I did manage to find out that the 'Private Room' was indeed situated somewhere in the back of the restaurant. The waiter told me so, and kindly showed me the way.

The *Fremdenzimmer* was large and sombre, furnished in the style of a gentlemen's club; the furniture was heavy and dark. A man rose from a large armchair and came toward me. He stood upright, stretching to his full height under the dim light filtering in from the window. He was tall, upright, and lean, but I didn't immediately see his face in the shadow; my eyes weren't yet accustomed to the gloom.

He scrutinised me in silence for a while.

'I don't know you,' he said curtly. But I wasn't rattled; I had carefully considered how I would tackle this difficult task.

'There's a man who is very interested in this meeting,' I said. 'He asked me to come in his place.'

He continued to inspect me. Now I could see his brown, smooth, expressionless face. His mouth formed a straight line like a cut across his face. It was handsome and symmetrical, but hard, with narrow, pale, blank eyes. His age was impossible to determine.

'You are a foreigner?' he stated brusquely.

'Yes – Finnish.'

He said something I didn't understand. Surely the adventure had begun; perhaps he was questioning me in Finnish. I flushed with embarrassment.

'I'm Swedish–Finnish,' I added.

He laughed, loudly and unpleasantly.

'I thought this might be a trick', he said, about to continue, but at that moment the door opened behind me, and someone entered. I heard the footsteps, and I also saw that something had changed in my interrogator's eyes; there was a glint in them, a yellow glimmer like that of a predator.

I turned, and at that same instant heard the tap of a cane. The man entering used a walking stick – it was the limping man. He was slightly below average height, and there was something meticulous about his appearance. His clothing was elegant, his movements studied and measured, and his gaze intelligent, cold, and probing. There was a deliberate air about him. He stopped in the centre of the room and studied the other man for a long time, paying no attention to me.

Then he extended his hand, but the other man did not take it. He let it fall.

'You haven't changed much over the years,' he said simply, with a shrug.

'You were wishing for that?' snapped the other. 'You hoped to find me unchanged? Well, by God, you're mistaken!'

'I neither hope nor expect anything,' replied the newcomer evenly, taking a seat in one of the armchairs. 'I wasn't the one who called this meeting. What do you want? I was going to ask you where you've been all these years, but you seem rather unfriendly,' he added.

The other composed himself with effort.

'Siberia, China, Outer Mongolia, China again,' he replied curtly.

'And now you've decided to gather the old guard?' continued the man in the armchair unperturbed. 'I assume you're the one behind the call in the *War Comrades Broadcast* and the papers?'

'There seems to be very few of us left,' he went on, continuing the conversation when the other merely nodded. But he didn't relent; gesturing toward me, he asked 'And who, by the way, is this?'

His question was never answered, for at that moment, the door opened again and a young lady appeared. She paused at the threshold, uncertain whether she should enter. She was tall and slender, dressed in a chic light–grey dress. Her hat was large and red, and beneath it shone a pale face, a pair of wide blue eyes, and a cherry–red mouth. She looked from one man to the other, and finally turned to the one in the armchair:

'Is it here,' she asked, 'where I can learn what happened in Olesko on the thirteenth of December, 1918?'

The man in the armchair stood politely.

'I'm sorry,' he said, 'but I'm not in charge of this gathering. I can only refer you to Herr Kunz Soten. He was a common hussar in Olesko back then. What he's since become in the Far East, I don't know, and so can't provide him with whatever title he may rightly bear. You see,' he said with ironic detachment, 'unfortunately, I lost track of him after that.'

And he pointed to the stranger who still stood directly across from me.

But Soten did not immediately respond. His eyes once again took on that strange, yellow glint, and he answered softly, slowly:

'Perhaps it will comfort you, von Winterstein, to know that I have not lost sight of you.'

He stood waiting, as though expecting a reaction. Von Winterstein shrugged. 'I get the impression that you hate me for some reason.'

Soten let out a high–pitched laugh.

It was distinctly unpleasant. The atmosphere in the dark room turned tense, harsh, and hostile. I felt no connection to what was unfolding; I understood none of it. I was simply there, like another object in the room. The earlier sense of unreality returned; I wished that I were more receptive, like when I was young. With age, you start to drift outside reality. You aren't always quivering with energy – not from early morning until late at night – and I caught myself wondering whether perhaps the Moselle wine I'd drunk earlier had something to do with it …

But Soten's voice interrupted my musings.

'You're right; I am in charge of this affair,' he continued. 'And I shall fully meet your expectations, Herr von Winterstein, you can count on it. Let's begin with a roll call. I have no list, but my memory is most reliable. I remember absolutely everything. And should I forget something, I'm sure you'll be able to help me …'

The young woman interjected, repeating her question. 'I responded to a call in the radio broadcast and newspapers to come here, believing I might learn more about the village of Olesko in Podolia, where something occurred on the 13th of December 1918. Was I mistaken?'

'Under certain conditions,' replied the man called Kunz Soten, 'you may indeed learn something.'

He brushed his forehead and began: 'Nine German and Austrian cavalrymen rode into Olesko on the evening of 13 December. They were Schneckenburger … Boehm, Mayer … Schulz, Winterstein, Krauter … Mendel—'

'My father was named Mendel,' interrupted the young woman. 'Frantz Mendel. My name is Eva – Eva Mendel.'

' … Steiner and myself,' continued Soten.

'I represent Steiner,' I interjected quickly, but Soten ignored me and turned to Winterstein.

'So, you see, only four have appeared; now you must help me. Weren't there more?'

'No,' said Winterstein. 'You said nine riders, and you've named them all.'

'There were eleven,' Soten said darkly. 'Eleven reached Olesko that evening.'

'Eleven?' Winterstein repeated.

'Yes,' said Soten, loudly and piercingly. 'I've a surprise for you. I intend to present the tenth rider; it will be a reunion …'

And with a dramatic flourish, he flung open the door to the inner room. A new man immediately appeared in the doorway; a gaunt, bony figure. I caught a glimpse of a tall, square forehead, a regular and rather handsome face marred by a large scar along the left jaw. His hair was greying at the temples, and his eyes — his eyes caught my attention — they were deep–set, intense, and flickering in a ravaged face where every feature seemed carved with a chisel.

Winterstein had risen to his feet, pale as a sheet. His eyes bulged like marbles; he was visibly shaken. He could not compose himself; clearly, this was something for which he had not been prepared.

'Jan,' he stammered, '—Jan …'

For a moment, he stood frozen like a statue. Soten's face gleamed with devilish delight. Then Winterstein spoke again, thick–voiced: 'But the eleventh rider; you said there were eleven riders who entered Olesko that evening.'

It was the new man who answered from the doorway. His voice was deep and slow.

'The eleventh rider who rode into Olesko that evening is also among us now. For the eleventh rider was Satan!'

A minute's silence followed, the retort still reverberating in the air. No one said anything, but Miss Mendel and I were complete outsiders; we may as well have been invisible to the others. We shared a furtive glance, sensing somehow that we shared a common fate in this strange reckoning which neither of us understood. She was the first to regain her composure. She resumed the conversation, and there was a note of restrained impatience in her voice as she continued:

'My father died in Olesko on the 13th of December 1918. He was found dead by Austrian troops who entered the town the next day. They discovered his diary …'

These words drew the others' attention. Everyone looked at her.

'A diary', Winterstein blurted out.

'Thank God,' said the man in the doorway.

Soten said nothing.

'Yes, a diary,' she repeated. 'Most soldiers kept diaries, didn't they?'

'Do you have it with you?' asked Soten quickly.

'Yes, I thought it best to bring it.'

'Well then,' Soten continued, glancing around, 'does anyone here object to us reading from Frantz Mendel's account of what happened in Olesko on the 13th of December?'

'But there's nothing in the diary,' said Eva Mendel apologetically. 'That's why I came. The diary ends on the 12th of December; or rather, my father added the heading: *Olesko, 13 December*, but there is no text beneath it. That's why I believe he died that day. The diary does show he had been wounded a few days earlier.'

Soten nodded. 'He took a bullet in the shoulder as we crossed a bridge, and he had a bit of wound fever, but nothing life–threatening …'

'How did he die, then?' she asked quietly.

Soten did not respond immediately. Instead, Winterstein spoke up:

'Your father died a soldier's death,' he said briskly. 'We were separated during the night. Those were turbulent times; half of Podolia was in the hands of the Reds, and we had to fight our way from place to place.'

'I believe we may have more to tell Miss Mendel later,' Soten said then. 'For now, perhaps it's best if the three of us continue the conversation. May I have your address?' he asked, and she handed him her card.

Then he turned to me. 'Where does Steiner live?'

I wasn't sure whether, after all that had happened, I was doing the right thing. But Adrian had impressed upon me, in no uncertain terms, never to reveal his whereabouts. So I simply handed over the letter of authorisation and added that his address was in Helsinki. Soten made a note of it, then he turned back to the other two.

'To return to the matter at hand – which, given the present circumstances, concerns only the three of us – I suggest that we continue alone.'

'Perhaps the other two might wait in the adjoining room,' Winterstein interjected. 'We may yet have need of them.'

Jan gave a subtle nod and opened the door for Eva Mendel and me to the room that had concealed him earlier in the meeting. I checked the time; it was now quarter to five. The meeting had taken its time, and it wasn't yet over. For now, we were confined – the young German girl with painted lips and myself, Valdemar Wiig, agricultural machinery merchant from Oslo – waiting to see what would unfold behind the closed door. I had gleaned some information; I had heard and noted a few names. I knew that the matter concerned Adrian somehow, that he had been in Olesko on a particular date, and that something important was tied to that event. But what? My task was not yet complete. I had to try and learn more.

'They're hiding something from us,' I whispered to the young woman. 'Do you understand any of this?'

She shook her head.

'I don't normally resort to such methods,' I continued, 'but the end justifies the means; let's try to follow along.'

I pulled two chairs close to the door. We sat with our ears pressed to the wood. Eva Mendel wore a dry, unusual perfume; or perhaps it was her powder that gave off such a strong scent. It distracted me somewhat and made it hard to concentrate; I wasn't used to situations like this. Fate had thrown me together with a young stranger, and now we were pressed up against a door so closely that I could clearly feel it. I saw the powder dusting her nose, and a coquettish glint in her eyes told me she was also aware of the moment. Her arm brushed against mine … Behind the closed door, we heard the murmur of muted voices. It was impossible to distinguish individual words; only a faint hum could be heard.

We sat that way for a long time.

Suddenly, we looked at one another, and I saw in her eyes the same astonishment that I felt. We had caught an incomprehensible phrase, a question. A voice, fanatical in tone, had risen, and another had immediately hushed it.

The question had been:

'But where is she? I want to know where she is.'

We had both heard it.

One more incident from that meeting must be mentioned; or rather, a scandal that occurred immediately afterwards. It made a deep impression on me, as it was the first time I had ever witnessed anything of the sort. The door was opened for us; we had, fortunately, drawn our chairs away in good time, and no one seemed to suspect us. We received a brief message: for now, nothing could be disclosed. The meeting was over, plain and simple. We would receive further information in writing. Soten's voice was icy, Winterstein's face red, and the man called Jan said nothing.

We left together through the restaurant. Winterstein walked a few steps ahead of the rest of us. It was then that the scandal happened. I had been thinking about Adrian's instruction that I must now ensure no one followed me or discovered where I was headed. In passing, I had noticed four men near the entrance dressed in brown SA uniforms; they were fairly loud. How it all began, I don't quite know; I was thinking of other things. But suddenly, one of the four addressed Soten sharply, asking why he had not returned his greeting. Soten responded curtly, and the man rose to his feet.

The next moment, a beer mug flew towards Soten's head, but he dodged it with lightning speed. What followed was a few seconds of indescribable chaos. I was shoved aside by someone and nearly toppled over a table, but otherwise came to no harm. Through the confusion – shouting, indignant voices, and waiters dashing about in panic – I noticed that all four of the men had thrown themselves at Soten, who, with a sudden movement, broke free and launched his own counterattack. Jan had stepped in beside him; those two rose up like a wall, calm yet unyielding and swift.

I remained completely passive. My knees were shaking; the impact was too sudden, too unexpected, too violent. I didn't come to their aid; besides, it wasn't my affair. For a few brutal seconds, I heard the dull sound of fists hitting flesh, a couple of bodies crashing to the ground, a table overturning, the splintering of wood … For a split second, I glimpsed the flash of a revolver's barrel, but a kick sent the hand holding the weapon flying upwards, and a muffled shot went off into the ceiling. I caught the acrid scent of gunpowder in the air …

Then suddenly it was all over. I saw the four uniformed men fleeing toward the entrance. Three of them managed to escape onto the square, but the fourth was too slow; the doorman tackled him, and the next moment, the *Schupo* appeared in the doorway. Two policemen in blue uniforms burst in, hands on their holsters, and in a flash, the doorman's captive was helpless in their grip and led back into the restaurant. They were polite but firm. 'You'll have to remain here for the time being,' they told him. 'We need to find out what happened.'

For a moment, the entrance was clear. I saw my chance to slip away without being followed. I was frightened and agitated and perhaps didn't fully consider what I was doing; I just had a desperate urge to get away from it all. I had my return ticket in my pocket and the train was waiting. So swiftly, and without anyone noticing, I made my way to the door and, in a moment, was out on the street. I avoided the direct route across the square toward the railway station and turned instead into a narrow alley to the right. In the next side street, I turned left and paused on the corner to listen. No one was following me. I continued down a couple more streets – right, then left – and paused again.

That's when I saw, down a narrow lane, a parked car, and beside it, a figure I recognised. It was Winterstein. He was speaking with someone inside the car, and what I saw next surprised me. It seemed clear that the people he was talking to were wearing brown uniforms …

I stood half–hidden in a gateway. No one could see me. I took my time and put on my glasses to be sure. It was true; inside the car, I could clearly see *S.A.* uniforms. Whether they were the same three from the restaurant, I couldn't say; they were too far away.

I remained in Berlin for a few more days. I knew no one and felt lonely. I wandered about the city all day long, visiting museums and art galleries in the morning, theatres and restaurants in the evening. One night, a red–haired hostess came and sat next to me in a bar. I told her I wanted to be left alone.

The next day, I travelled north towards Sassnitz and the Baltic Sea. At the station, I bought some newspapers; among them was the *Kölnische Zeitung*. A notice on the front page immediately caught my attention, and I'll reproduce it here in full, as it related directly to the incident at the restaurant.

The headline read: '**Provocateurs at Large.**'

The text continued:

'The affair previously reported concerning the assault in the "Heilige Lampe" has now reached its preliminary summary judgement in court. It has been established that neither of the two assaulted gentlemen gave the slightest provocation for the incident. Furthermore, it has been incontrovertibly proven that the four assailants did not belong to any official S.A. formation, and that therefore they wore the uniform illegally. The three who managed to escape are still being sought by police, but it is believed they left Cologne immediately. The fourth, who was apprehended, is a repeat offender with several previous convictions for violent behaviour. Yesterday, he was sentenced to six months in prison for assault and four years for the unauthorised and provocative use of a uniform, the court considering his record and the nature of his actions to be particularly damaging to the reputation of the uniform he impersonated. The court further concluded that this was a premeditated provocation.'

I let the newspaper fall to my lap.

CHAPTER III

And so, I was back at Hasselbakken; I had sent a telegram and was expected. I took a car immediately and arrived just half an hour after the train pulled in. We no longer sat around the fireplace; we had moved outside and were gathered on the veranda. Before us lay the village, scattered with farms, white villas, and gardens full of lilac; behind it, peaceful, wooded hills arched gently into the sky. The night air was mild and clear, showing every detail for our appreciation; nothing is so white and fragrant with light as a Nordic summer night. Far off, on the edge of the forest, a lone cuckoo called.

I had taken the liberty of kissing Anne Marie's hand and told her that this had become a habit of mine after eight days abroad. She had teased me for my short absence.

'You'll never amount to anything,' she said. 'You're a hopeless bachelor, tragically sticking to routine. There you were, off abroad with the means and freedom to stay away a while, and yet you immediately turned your nose homeward. Next time, I'll come along to look after you.'

'Yes, thank you,' I replied. 'But let it be soon.'

'So you weren't scared off by your trip?' Adrian asked, pressing my hand meaningfully.

'On the contrary,' I said. 'It was quite a splendid journey. I enjoyed myself thoroughly.'

I understood that he was burning to hear my account; he was restless, impatient, unable to sit still. He paced the floor and disturbed us; we couldn't settle into our usual easy conversation. I knew the reason, but could do nothing about it. Anne Marie had to be kept out of it; that was his rule, not mine. In the end, Anne

Marie and I did most of the talking. Adrian couldn't interrupt; the serenity of the summer night stood by us. I sat watching a small cloud that hovered in the pale sky. It didn't move; it hung there, waiting for sunrise and the morning breeze.

Naturally, they asked for details of my journey. Again, it was Anne Marie who led the questioning. Adrian was cautious, afraid I might touch on the secret assignment. I spoke of this and that, all the trivial things that happen while travelling. I talked of Berlin; the museums and theatres, the elegant cars, and massive new buildings. I had also been to the Avus track for a motor race …

Then Anne Marie teased me again about my swift return, but was suddenly interrupted by Adrian.

'Oh, do be quiet for once,' he burst out. 'No one finds you funny.'

'What's the matter with you?' she asked, surprised. 'He's been like this lately,' she turned to me, 'irritable and nervous. Since you left, he's not been himself; he's been impossible to live with. I'm honestly glad you came back so soon, you know. You mustn't go away again.'

'You're exaggerating,' he said. 'and repeating yourself. It's not amusing.'

But Anne Marie brushed off his sulkiness with elegant flair. 'Valdemar,' she said, 'you decide. Wasn't I funny?'

'What Anne Marie does,' I replied, referring to her in the third person and trying to stay neutral, 'is not something one can rightly criticise. She is beyond reproach.'

'You should be married to her,' Adrian muttered, trying to play it off as a joke. But I was irritated with his moodiness and decided to tease him a little to toy with his tension. It was perhaps unkind, but he had it coming.

'It's true,' I said suddenly. 'Something *did* happen. I forgot to mention that I made a quick trip to Cologne, and had a little adventure in a restaurant called *Heilige Lampe*.'

Adrian jolted in his seat and coughed uncomfortably; he didn't have time to kick me under the table.

'Tell us,' said Anne Marie with a smile. 'Tell us about your restaurant adventure. Was it a girl?'

'No, a fight,' I said. 'A proper, full–blown brawl.'

Adrian stared at me open–mouthed, trying to signal me to stop, but I pretended not to notice and continued my little revenge. I felt I'd done well, so had earned the right to keep him on edge. Besides, I was defending Anne Marie.

I recounted the incident, described the brawl itself, but carefully withheld everything else. I didn't mention the meeting, nor that I knew the two men who were attacked. I acted as though I had simply been a bystander, which, in a sense, was true.

'But what caused it?' Adrian asked anxiously. 'Surely there must have been some kind of trigger?' He forgot entirely that Anne Marie was still present.

'Well, yes,' I replied indifferently. 'There was probably some sort of trigger …'

Adrian sat as if on hot coals. 'You must be tired after the journey,' he suggested suddenly. I knew exactly what he was implying.

But the summer night was so gentle; a white mist had settled over the landscape, veiling the distant church tower. There was a whisper in the forest and meadows; the cuckoo had fallen silent.

'Yes,' I said. 'I suppose I should be tired.'

Anne Marie glanced sideways at me; I felt it more than saw it. She sat in her deckchair, wearing a large plain straw hat. Her dress was floral, and beneath it, a slender ankle flicked beneath a white stocking.

CHAPTER III

It was the last peaceful evening at Hasselbakken.

Adrian insisted on accompanying me on the way home; he said he wanted to take a short evening walk. Naturally, I understood his intentions.

'Well then' he said, expectantly, once we had gone a little way down the slope. 'Tell me, who did you meet?'

We sat down on a moss–covered stone wall; the forest stood lush around us, and far away we could hear the hum of the occasional car on the main road.

'It was a man named Kunz Soten behind it all,' I said, and noted that this information seemed to surprise Adrian.

'But Wint … I mean the lame man,' he quickly corrected himself.

'You mean Winterstein,' I said calmly. 'Yes, he and Soten didn't appear to be particularly good friends.'

Adrian's secrecy and lack of trust began to annoy me. After all, I had done him a favour by making the journey. He didn't need to keep Winterstein's name from me; I couldn't understand what difference it could make. In a way, my curiosity had also been stirred. I felt I had acquired some ownership over the entire affair, having learned more about it through my journey; this, combined with my irritation, gave me the impulse to test Adrian a little.

'No,' said Adrian, and laughed joylessly, 'I can well imagine that Soten and Winterstein were not friends.'

'Soten was there from the beginning,' I continued. 'Then I arrived, then Winterstein, and then Eva Mendel …'

'Eva Mendel?'

'She's the daughter of Frantz Mendel, who fell in Olesko on the 13th of December 1918,' I informed him.

Adrian looked at me and said nothing. I went on: 'But at the end, the tenth rider arrived—'

'Tenth rider?'

'Yes; didn't eleven German and Austrian horsemen ride into Olesko?' I asked innocently.

Adrian thought for a long time.

'We were nine,' he said finally.

'But Jan?' I tossed in casually.

Adrian started and turned toward me in great agitation.

'What do you mean by that?' he asked sharply. 'What does Jan have to do with this; explain yourself!'

'My dear fellow,' I said coolly, 'I believe I mentioned that the tenth rider appeared at Heilige Lampe.'

'Jan,' Adrian whispered in a broken voice, 'Jan – no, it can't be true …' He nearly collapsed there on the stone wall. His hands began to tremble; it was almost a small breakdown right before my eyes. But after a while, he collected himself and asked in a somewhat calm voice:

'Can you describe him for me?'

I did so as well as I could.

'He may, of course, have changed over the years,' Adrian muttered to himself, 'but quite a few things match.'

'It seemed', I added with feigned indifference, 'that Winterstein was very surprised to see Jan; he evidently wasn't expecting it.'

In my quiet mind, I thought it odd that this man's appearance should make such a strong impression on both Adrian and Winterstein; there must be something behind it. Jan had behaved considerably more calmly during the meeting than Kunz Soten.

Adrian continued: 'What did Jan say, how did he behave?'

Then I decided to drop my big bomb and observe the reaction.

'Jan said little,' I replied, 'But in the end, he asked a question; I happened to overhear it. "Where is she?" he asked. 'I want to know where she is!"

But Adrian didn't react to that – perhaps he had already pulled himself together – and I got nothing out of my observation. He offered me a cigarette and lit his own with a hand that trembled slightly.

'You'll have to start from the beginning and tell it all in order,' he said.

We sat for a long time; the first golden stripe already stretched across the eastern sky by the time I had finished. Adrian sat silent for a long time; he seemed relieved. He thanked me and extended his hand.

'So I'm in the background,' he said at last. 'You're sure no one followed you?'

I nodded.

'What do you make of it all?' Adrian asked.

'In the absence of your trust,' I said bitterly, 'my impression is naturally very patchy. But if you're interested, I can say this. I believe the following points are clear: Something happened in Olesko on a specific date, and only a few insiders know about it. These insiders were summoned via an advertisement, and Soten was behind the invitation, who had been away for a long time and so didn't know where the others were now living. In some way, he was in contact with Jan; at least, he knew Jan was hidden in the side room. What actually happened in Olesko on the thirteenth of December 1918, I of course don't know; but I would be very interested to find out, since I'm frankly a little touched by your lack of trust in me. It's obvious it's important, otherwise no one would be going to such trouble to bring the matter back up after so many years. I've gathered enough to know that, in some way, it's connected to a woman.'

Adrian nodded thoughtfully, but gave me no confidence in return.

Suddenly I remembered the notice in *Kölnische Zeitung*. I took the clipping from my wallet and handed it to him. Adrian read it carefully.

'That's Winterstein's doing,' he said, handing it back. 'Winterstein is still the same. They'll chase each other to death.'

It was as though that thought didn't particularly trouble him. I understood Adrian less and less. The golden–red stripe on the sky grew with every passing minute. A bird awoke and began to sing, but stopped suddenly, since it was still night.

Now it's time I spoke about my telescope, which played a crucial role the next day. The same uncle who left me his machinery business also left me a Zeiss telescope, an excellent instrument that I have greatly enjoyed. From my veranda I have a view over the whole village, and I can follow the cars speeding along the road. Once on a walk, I paced out a two–kilometre distance between two points that I can see from my veranda. Since then, I've been able to sit and follow the cars with the telescope between those two points; it's quite fun, especially when I have the clock in front of me.

When a car takes less than a minute on the stretch, I mutter to myself: 'There's another damned speedster.' Once after a car accident, I was able to help the police this way. From my veranda I can also see the fjord and follow the large steamers on their journey; I can make out the sloops and the white sails. My excellent telescope helps pass the time, and I can also see Hasselbakken quite clearly.

Adrian was due to perform the next day. I sat on my veranda and watched him walk down towards the railway station. I let the telescope drift toward Hasselbakken, but Anne Marie was nowhere to be seen. Nor did she accompany Adrian, as she sometimes did; she was likely at home, busy with something. The afternoon sun burned down, the air hot and dry. I saw Adrian stop and wipe his forehead with his handkerchief. My telescope was good; I could even discern the expression on his face, as he was quite close. Then I let the telescope drift further; following a lorry along the road, a dog scampered past, a cyclist glided over the asphalt, and a man was walking on the main road. He carried a heavy suitcase; he set it down a couple of times and took out his handkerchief. He was struggling with it, poor fellow, and on top of it all, he was limping. A heavy suitcase in this heat – I didn't envy his task.

I let the telescope drift further out over the fjord, towards Oslo, and a distant plane caught my attention. Then I thought about Adrian again. He had come a long way down the hill; he was already halfway to the station. The road disappeared briefly behind some trees, and I directed the telescope to the other side where I expected him to reappear. Then suddenly, a new figure appeared in the field of view; it was the man with the suitcase. He was walking up toward Hasselbakken and disappeared into the trees where I knew Adrian was headed downwards. The limping man with the heavy suitcase … A chill passed through me. Could it be possible? *Nonsense*, I told myself, *you're seeing ghosts, the journey has gotten to you! In a moment, Adrian will appear again …* And I kept the telescope fixed on the cluster of trees.

But nothing happened. The minutes passed. No one appeared. Adrian and the limping man must be somewhere behind those trees. Any other explanation was impossible. I could clearly see the road on both sides and the boundary stones; I also knew there was no sunken path there. Now the train was departing as well; Adrian would be late for his rehearsal. It was unlike him; he was always meticulously punctual with his work. My unease turned to certainty, and my thoughts spun. What was happening behind that thicket, and what could I do?

Should I try to go over there? But I knew nothing; I had been kept out of the whole thing. I sat down again, but the next moment I wondered whether something terrible might be happening over there. 'Winterstein is still the same,' Adrian had said, with a sinister implication to his words.

The minutes passed. I looked at the clock; half an hour had gone by. Finally, just as my anxiety peaked and I had decided to telephone Anne Marie, something happened. They both came into view, but they were walking up towards Hasselbakken. Adrian was carrying the suitcase.

So it *was* Winterstein. Nothing else could have made Adrian abandon his rehearsal; he had likely telephoned now and said he'd suddenly become ill. Now all that unknown – the suffering and hatred from Heilige Lampe, the mystery from the other day and Olesko – had suddenly drawn close to us.

'They'll chase each other to death,' Adrian had said. These were desperate people who still had the war in their nerves; they thought and felt differently from us. I recalled their violent behaviour during the fight and involuntarily shuddered. And now, caught in the middle of it all, was the gentle Adrian. And Anne Marie.

But what could I do?

I sat thinking for a long time. And I concluded that I, too, would have to throw myself into this game; I had to come to their aid in one way or another. Adrian had his hands tied, and Anne Marie knew nothing. I weighed the options, discarding plans as they emerged.

Then the telephone rang. It was Adrian. He was very agitated, nearly beside himself; he spoke conspicuously softly, as if afraid someone might overhear him.

'It's me,' he said, 'I can't mention names, but the lame man …' he almost whispered, 'the lame man has suddenly arrived. For Anne Marie's sake, the two of you must not meet. You understand; she mustn't suspect anything about Heilige Lampe. So you must be kind enough not to visit us for a while. I'll let you know as soon as the coast is clear …'

'Is there nothing I can do to help you?' I asked.

'No. I must manage this alone, don't misunderstand.'

'I can surely mention a name here on the phone?' I asked.

'Of course—'

'It's Winterstein, then—'

'Yes.'

'But how did he find you? Did he have your address?'

Adrian's voice was bitter and full of sarcasm as he answered:

'Your immense cunning in Cologne didn't help us much. He simply telephoned your description to Berlin, and when you arrived, you were followed from the station to your hotel, where you handed your passport to the porter. That's how he learned you were Norwegian. That was enough for him. He also kept informed about your departure date and knew where you were headed.'

'But how did he find out where you lived?'

'You don't know him,' Adrian still whispered. 'Everything's easy for him. He knew I was a decent musician. When he arrived in Oslo, he merely asked the hotel porter to get him some photos of local orchestras; he said he was here to arrange some engagements. He found me right away. He would have found me even if I'd been living alone in some remote valley; it wouldn't have helped. But now we must end this …'

'Yes, but remember, if there's anything I can do—'

'Thank you, I'll remember,' said Adrian, and hung up.

'Give my regards to Anne Marie—' I said into the receiver, but of course, that was foolish, since he couldn't.

There was my rescue mission quite thoroughly dismissed, and on top of that, I had learnt I'd nearly made a mess of things! But I had only followed my instructions; Adrian hadn't foreseen that I could be watched in Berlin, and from his words it was clear that Winterstein would likely have found him anyway.

The days passed. I bitterly regretted not having stayed in Germany; I felt even more alone here with my telescope and Hasselbakken in view. A couple of times I saw all three of them go out for a walk. Sometimes I was tempted to do the same and 'accidentally' run into them. I still had my freedom of movement, after all; but when I imagined how Winterstein would smile and say *aha, it's our friend from Heilige Lampe — guten Tag, Herr Ekki Muller!* I gave it up. I had also played a false game with Anne Marie, 'or aided in it', as the lawyers say.

The days passed. One evening I tuned my radio to foreign broadcasts and first got some music, but then there followed a dull rumble. I wasn't paying attention to what was being announced and at first thought it was electrical interference, but then my ear caught a certain rhythm, and I began to make out the individual sounds.

It was marching columns; infantry with heavy, rhythmic, hobnailed boots, cavalry with clattering, dancing hooves, cannons rolling heavily over cobblestones, motorcars, motorcycles, and transport. An army on the march. In between came fiery, sharp military marches, rising, peaking, fading away, receding; now and then came a soldier's song. Then again the heavy footsteps, hooves clattering, cannons rolling; dull booms were heard, and the angry trebles of machine guns rang out. Hell was let loose. And suddenly, a grave voice rang out over it all and recited to this gigantic audio accompaniment:

Kamerad, wo bist du? …

Comrade, where are you?

That was the overture. Then followed the 'comrade search' in rapid succession, like so many small, living sketches from the world conflagration seventeen years ago; pictures drawn straight from life and death at the time.

CHAPTER III

Do you remember, comrade, an episode on the slope at the Somme on 1 April, 1917; you must remember it if you're alive, for you took a bullet through your arm then. Write to me, my address is …

Hello, I've often thought of you, comrade, and of that time we carried the dead Lieutenant Seyfert out of the line of fire near Bapaume …

Comrade, did you make it? We escaped together from the POW camp near Tobolsk on 16 May, 1916; we were separated in the dark, the guards shot at us. If you're alive, come to me, I'm well off, I live at …

Ghosts, ghosts …

Memories and yet more memories of the time when the Juggernaut rolled across the globe and crushed millions of fates into dust; memories of death and blood and sacrifice, memories of dry, burning tears. But through it all, like a tiny beam of light, rose the human will to live, to find comfort and warmth and a spark of the eternal fire. Like the heather seed swirling in the storm and finding a poor mountain crevice filled with everlasting ice and barren stone, and yet taking root, so rose a spark of life from Ragnarök and shone like a halo in Hell: **Comrade, where are you – the sacred, eternal, indestructible camaraderie.**

It was eerie and harrowing. I sat there and couldn't help but think of another broadcast, another search that would recently have passed through the same programme slot, which must have sounded something like this:

Comrade, where are you – on the 13th of December 1918, nine riders rode into Olesko – do you remember, comrade …

But there was something threatening and grim about this appeal; here, there was no warmth, no spark of humanity's sacred fire. And vaguely, as through a veil, I sensed Jan's hollow voice: **The eleventh rider was Satan …**

There had to be a terrible, deep secret binding the comrades from Olesko together.

CHAPTER IV

You can sometimes influence your fate, while remaining loyal to it. I managed it thanks to my telescope. One day Anne Marie was walking alone down the road from Hasselbakken, heading toward the small cluster of buildings around the station that marks the commercial area. I suddenly remembered that I was out of cigarettes.

'Good day,' said Anne Marie, 'I thought you were dead.'

'No,' I replied sheepishly, 'I've just been busy.'

'—Or a bit jealous of our German guest?' she continued mercilessly, 'yes, of course you know we have a German guest!'

'I've heard about it,' I said carefully, and added: 'Who is he?'

'He's one of Adrian's war comrades,' said Anne Marie, 'and he's a very cultivated and well–read man; apparently he has a reputation as an art historian. His name is Kunicke – Doctor Kunicke.'

It gave me a jolt. Once again, I had found the mystery; why was this Winterstein using a false name? My confusion and my guilt increased, but I could say nothing; I was bound to silence, and there was Anne Marie, unaware …

'Shall we take advantage of this lovely weather for a walk?' she asked. 'Do you have time?'

'Of course,' I replied, 'time is the only thing I always have enough of.'

And we walked uphill toward the large white manor that lies on the ridge, surrounded by ancient pagan sacrificial groves of ash and oak; the roads were white with dust and the early summer worker, the dandelion, was in brazen bloom along every roadside and had invaded every field. To our left a lake glinted, then the forests stretched for miles inward, ridge after ridge always northward toward the country's heart.

'Will Doctor Kunicke be staying with you long?' I asked cautiously.

'He lives with us,' said Anne Marie, 'he seems to have settled in for good. I don't understand what's gotten into Adrian; he won't budge on the matter. I've said the man could stay at a hotel; by all accounts, he's a wealthy man. But Adrian says no, that's out of the question – it's an old war comrade, he says – we must take care of him, he's alone in the world, and he's expecting to live with us. Women can't understand these things, Adrian says; one must have experienced the war to grasp the bond that still ties us from those days. Besides, he had already invited him to stay, so the matter was settled. And now he's moved in—' Anne Marie spoke with strained cheerfulness, '—and made himself quite cosy. We've had electricians in for two days. Kunicke has gout and needs special electrical equipment, a sort of enhanced sunlamp, he told me. Yes, I'm graciously allowed to use the device whenever I want, but thank God we have enough natural sunlight now—'

'So you won't get the benefit until autumn or winter,' I remarked.

'Yes, as you can see, cheerful prospects; I've basically been overthrown in my own home. Today Adrian told me that Doctor Kunicke would like to keep a dog; he's an animal lover, he said. I didn't reply, but instead addressed Kunicke directly and said that I could not have a dog in my house; I can't stand them, I said, I get ill from dogs, I must leave the house if a dog even comes into the neighbourhood. You know that's not true, but it had the desired effect.'

'So he's staying in the guest room?' I asked.

'Yes, in the veranda room. It's been redone for him; that's where he's installed all his electrical devices. And there he and Adrian sit, talking for hours on end; honestly, I prefer not to disturb them. But Adrian is not himself anymore.'

'This all sounds completely absurd,' I exclaimed, upset.

'Oh yes,' said Anne Marie in a light tone, 'it can go on for a while, of course. I will consider that this is Adrian's old war comrade. But then it'll be my turn …'

Her voice and manner were full of energy; I knew Anne Marie was a strong–willed woman. But at the same time, I had a discouraging feeling that something covert and murky was going on.

'You couldn't consider going away for a while?' I suggested gently.

'No,' said Anne Marie, tossing her head back so the sun glinted in her golden–red hair, 'I'm not running away from Kunicke.'

'That wasn't quite what I meant,' I said.

We continued walking; this was damned difficult.

'Look, Anne Marie,' I said after a while, 'can you see how the ridge looks like a resting troll; right behind the manor you can see the head, it sort of lies in the crook of its arm. Can you see it?'

Anne Marie stopped. 'Yes, indeed,' she said, 'it's rather funny. Isn't there a legend that a troll is supposed to live inside that ridge?'

'I've heard that too,' I said, and added randomly 'but sometimes trolls come to the people, Anne Marie, and then you have to be prepared.'

'What do you mean?' she asked, her attention piqued.

But my courage failed me, and I contented myself with that half–spoken remark. 'Well,' I said, 'shall we go on, or turn back?'

'You must come up to visit us one day,' said Anne Marie when we were about to part. 'You mustn't stay away from us. I miss you more than usual, given the way things are.'

'Couldn't we rather meet now and then and go for walks like today?' I suggested. 'This Doctor Kunicke …'

' ... is someone you can't tolerate,' Anne Marie continued and smiled at me. 'I shall give it serious thought. Farewell, and thank you for today.'

The sun shone more strongly than before, the roads were whiter, the dandelions more yellow.

—

'I can tell you something, but you mustn't say it to anyone,' said my landlady one day.

'Well,' I replied indifferently. I am used to her; she warrants a chapter for herself. She lives for others and through others' experiences. She knows everything that happens within a certain radius, but nothing outside of it. No one understands where she gets her knowledge from.

I've read that in the jungles of inner Africa, news spreads through the air in some inexplicable wireless fashion from tribe to tribe, faster than any tom–tom drum can beat. It's the same with my landlady; she's ahead of everyone else, she anticipates things almost before they occur, and she outpaces all human means of communication. She operates by instinct. But she's by no means one–sided, and she doesn't scorn ordinary mechanical means; I've caught her lifting the phone receiver and listening at random, hoping for a crossed line.

Usually, I couldn't care less about what she tells me, and I make that very clear, but it doesn't deter her.

'Arvid Falk is staying at the hotel,' she said.

That meant nothing to me; I didn't remember the name. She may have been irritated by my lack of interest. I usually respond with exaggerated indifference when she tries to draw me into the village's affairs.

'Arvid Falk, well,' she said, 'the detective.'

Then it dawned on me that I *had* heard of him. He was a younger member of the Falk family who had strayed from the beaten path. He was a lawyer, had worked as a crime reporter, and then set up in Oslo as a private detective. Falk had a good reputation and had attracted attention with a couple of cases.

'He's staying there under a false name,' whispered my landlady conspiratorially. 'He calls himself Arvid Beck.'

Another link in the chain; the thunderstorm was drawing closer. I knew Adrian knew Falk. He had once helped him with the legal formalities when Adrian became a Norwegian citizen.

'He's stayed there before,' my landlady continued, undeterred. 'That was when the major embezzlement was discovered, and they were afraid that office manager Stamseth might do something to himself; it's four years ago now.'

'How do you know everything, Mrs Strand?'

'Oh, this wasn't difficult; the landlady at the hotel told me. I only had to promise not to pass it on. She recognised Falk from back then.'

'Yes,' I said, to test her, 'what do you really think of this, Mrs Strand; do you think something is afoot?'

'There was certainly something afoot the last time he stayed there,' my landlady said.

'Maybe he's just resting a bit, taking a holiday, for instance?'

'Under a false name?' said Mrs Strand mockingly.

'No, no—' I admitted. 'But what could it be?'

I wanted to hear her opinion; surely nothing had leaked about Adrian's troubles.

'I know what I know,' said my landlady mysteriously; and that could not be denied. I didn't ask her anything further, and my tactic bore immediate fruit.

'I think it's murder—' she burst out, but what she meant by that, I didn't find out.

Still, I now understood more of the case, and Arvid Falk's arrival, as troubling as it might be, was at least a strengthening of the common front from which I was still excluded. For the first time, I was grateful to my gossip–loving landlady.

I kept a close eye on Hasselbakken. I examined every window with the telescope, and of course I paid special attention to the road; it was possible Anne Marie might set out for another walk. And this was how I made my next advance, and a discovery that struck me as so important that I immediately contacted Adrian and tried to pave my way into his confidence, despite having previously been denied it.

I was sitting with my telescope, studying Hasselbakken and its surroundings, when I saw something move in the background at the top of the roof. Behind Adrian's house lies a wooded rocky hill; the plot is blasted into the rock, and two metres behind the house a vertical rock wall rises. A bush moved violently, as if pushed aside, then all was still. I methodically scanned the surroundings and tried to distinguish between light and shadow, and suddenly, I had it!

Two faces clearly emerged somewhere in the shade under a spruce tree; there was no room for doubt, I saw them move, then they disappeared. They retreated up the hill; two figures, now and then hidden from me behind trees and brush, then emerging again. They moved to the other side of the house, and again they stopped. There was no doubt they were doing their best not to be seen from the house. They were observing it, noting windows and doors; their method was entirely cunning. There was little chance they would be noticed from inside, as their position was level with the roof. I turned hot and cold as I sat there; should I call and warn Adrian immediately?

On the other hand, I had the distinct impression that this was merely a reconnaissance; it seemed unlikely that any violence would be attempted in broad daylight. Better to wait, to prepare, and, if needed, notify the police.

Again, the two figures moved uphill, and this time they disappeared over the ridge; I saw them clearly silhouetted against a light clearing in the distance. Could it have been two vagrants? Of course, that possibility couldn't be ruled out. But Winterstein's arrival, his desire to keep a guard dog, and Arvid Falk's stay at the hotel all considered alongside my experiences at Heilige Lampe, pointed in a different direction.

Then my attention was once again caught. A third figure appeared on the ridge of the hill, moving cautiously from bush to bush, bent forward. There could be no doubt. *The third figure was following the other two.*

———

I telephoned Adrian and told him I had to speak with him. 'Excellent,' he said, 'you beat me to it; we were just talking about you today. I had been about to call and ask you to drop by. Do come over this evening.'

'It's too late,' I said. 'This is something important. I need to speak with you right away.'

'Then come for dinner,' said Adrian. 'You'll have to take what we've got.'

'Come and meet me,' I said, 'I'll leave here at exactly half past two.'

'OK,' Adrian replied.

He met me a bit down the hill. He was calm and contented, and his nervousness seemed to have lifted; did he suspect nothing? Or had the soldier Adrian returned; was this his true nature when something serious was at hand? I was thoroughly puzzled by my friend.

'While I remember,' he began at once, 'you mustn't mention Heilige Lampe at all. And you must refer to my guest as Kunicke; you must not slip up. He, for his part, will not mention that you've met before. He also knows your real name.'

'Adrian,' I said seriously and stopped walking, 'do you know your house is being watched by two mysterious people?'

The news had no impact on Adrian. He merely looked at me attentively and asked, 'How do you know?'

'I saw them this morning, through my telescope from my veranda.'

'Yes, I'm caught up in something, as you've no doubt realised,' said Adrian casually, 'and we must be prepared for all sorts of things. Your message doesn't surprise me.'

'Won't you alert the police?'

Adrian shook his head. 'No, not yet,' he said. 'We don't really know if anything is going to happen.'

'But do you know who these two fellows sneaking around are?'

'Yes,' said Adrian, 'it's Kunz Soten and Jan; they arrived in Norway last night.'

'But you must do something,' I said vehemently, 'for Anne Marie's sake you must act; you can't just sit around waiting for something to happen. Can't you at least go away?'

'Since you're so concerned for Anne Marie,' said Adrian, 'then you could, for instance, stay with us tonight; we can stay up through the night. Tomorrow evening, we can be together as well. Would that satisfy you?'

I didn't like his tone; it was the first time Adrian had addressed me in such a manner, and I was hurt, though I tried to hide it. 'Fine,' I said curtly, 'I accept your offer, but not in the spirit in which it was made.'

———

Anne Marie greeted me with a warm welcome. Winterstein – no, Kunicke – was reserved. I didn't like him. His eyes were cold and unfriendly, and even now there was something deliberate about him. He clearly had great influence over Adrian. He struck me as a man who lived in his own world and judged everything by his own peculiar standards. There was a cool calm about him; there was no room for doubt or uncertainty in his presence. And I saw in his eyes that Adrian was in his power and had regained only a semblance of calm thanks to that fact. Anne Marie seemed to notice the same; she was visibly irritated, almost hostile, not towards me, but the other two. She came and went, busy with her duties as hostess.

'Mr Wiig reports that he saw our two friends this morning,' said Adrian to Winterstein while Anne Marie was briefly out of the room.

Winterstein raised his eyebrows but said nothing.

'There was also a third,' I added, 'I forgot to mention that earlier. And they were following the other two.'

Winterstein studied me closely. I continued. The man irritated me; I wanted at least a moment of attention.

'By the way,' I said casually to Adrian, 'have you seen your friend Arvid Falk? He's staying at the hotel under the name Beck.'

It worked. Adrian didn't answer at once, but Winterstein asked instead how I had come by that information. I shrugged in return.

'You're remarkably well–informed,' said Winterstein thoughtfully, and his eyes didn't leave me. It was as if he was turning over a problem in his mind.

'No,' I said, 'I'm not; I just keep an eye on the things I can't help but see. And since I've ended up in this mess, I am curious about the next act.'

'And how far do you think we have come?' asked Winterstein, smiling faintly.

'The deployment is complete,' I said. 'The troops are in place; the game can begin.'

'You may be right,' said Winterstein, and gave a dry, unpleasant, gurgling laugh.

I felt as though he had analysed me through his half-lidded, indifferent eyes.

'You misunderstood me earlier,' said Adrian suddenly, 'I didn't mean to be unfriendly. By God, I have no reason to be. The thing is, we'd like you to stay with us until – until something happens. We have our reasons; we already talked about this before you called.'

'What are you expecting to happen?' I asked.

'I can't say; we can't be certain what the future will bring,' answered Adrian evasively.

'But you've seen for yourself how certain people are sneaking about.'

'Violence?' I asked.

Adrian shrugged.

'Do you have weapons?' I continued. 'I mean, I've got a revolver at home.'

Winterstein smiled. 'You don't need a revolver,' he said. 'We'll take care of that sort of thing. You're only here to see and hear and to be an unwilling witness to what unfolds; the less you know beforehand, the better. Besides, nothing's going to happen tonight; the other two need at least a day to prepare. They're unfamiliar with people and the place.'

For the second time, my role in this play had been reduced to watching and listening, but at least I was no longer on the outside. I was at the centre of the battlefield now with Anne Marie.

She called us to the table. It was a long afternoon, a long evening, and a long night.

Something new had entered Hasselbakken; a foreign presence had arrived. It was as if something had broken, and now we were stepping around shards and splinters. Clouds had gathered in the sky, but it didn't rain. The air had lost its freshness; it was muggy and oppressive. Outside in the dark, the unknown lurked; I could feel it, and I often glanced among the trees. At times, it seemed as if shadows vanished.

I noticed that Adrian, too, was restless now; when he spoke, he often paused to listen. Several times that evening, the phone rang, and each time he started violently. Once he returned and called for Winterstein, and they disappeared together into the hallway.

'What does all this mean?' asked Anne Marie in distress. 'Do you know anything?'

But I shook my head. 'Perhaps they're doing business together,' I said, just to say something.

—

I stayed longer than I ought, to be present if anything should happen. But all was quiet. When I left, I asked politely if they might visit me sometime – they said they'd be glad to – and strangely enough, Winterstein was particularly eager.

'What about tomorrow evening?' he suddenly asked out in the hallway. 'Would that suit you?'

'Perfectly,' I stammered, confused; I understood less than ever. Why did Winterstein have no objection to leaving Hasselbakken on the very evening he expected something to occur? Were they perhaps expecting a personal attack?

It was as if Winterstein had read my mind.

'Shall I walk with you part of the way?' he asked unexpectedly. 'Perhaps you find it unpleasant to walk alone?'

There was a hint of mockery in his tone.

'No — no thank you,' I replied angrily. But from the shadows of the bushes, I felt that white ghostly hands reached for me, and human shapes lurked among the branches — a large stone startled me terribly — the landscape was pale and strange compared to daytime. I ran the last stretch until I reached the main road, my heart pounding.

CHAPTER V

My landlady is quite capable of arranging things when she has enough time and sufficiently detailed instructions. She prepares the food according to my directions and handles the setup; the finishing touch, the final brushstroke, is my privilege.

You must always establish in advance the nature of a gathering, but this requires a good deal of psychological insight. I console myself with the fact that the parties I host are generally quite successful; this ability, which many have assured me I possess in abundance, comforts me and compensates for the somewhat modest contribution I make to Wiig & Westerberg.

With the events of the previous evening fresh in my mind, I had resolved to lift the mood right from the outset. The party was disjointed, we were running on five wheels, and each of us was weighed down by unrelated concerns. I decided to start with a cocktail, then a starter accompanied by ice–cold Linie aquavit. It was perhaps double sacrilege, and up for debate, but I went for it; the end justifies the means!

Winterstein looked around, completely at ease. His eyes swept over the interior and clearly said: the home of a wealthy idler, quite comfortable, a bit ordinary, a few decent pictures on the walls. Those interested him, and he regarded them like a connoisseur. I swallowed the rest of my cocktail. Without saying or doing anything at all, that man came across as one incessant insult.

The air was stifling again that day; our clammy faces and hands glowed, and it was hard to breathe. The alcohol made us feel even warmer, but in return freed us somewhat from the discomfort. We no longer noticed it so sharply; for a while, we were in rather good spirits.

'Dr Kunicke must surely know the bust of that Egyptian queen you spoke about from Berlin, the one that made such an impression on you …' said Anne Marie.

'Nefertiti,' I said. 'The bust is in the Egyptian department of the Neues Museum, I spent several mornings in front of it. I couldn't tear myself away; I stood there for hours.'

Winterstein looked at me with a strange glint in his cold eyes, then he raised his glass towards the light and watched the play of the wine's colour.

'Strange,' he said, 'wherever I travel in the world – and I've travelled a great deal – I always run into fanatical admirers of Nefertiti. This beautiful dead queen still has, more than three thousand years after her death, a circle of worldwide friends, worshippers, even lovers. That's the impression she's made. One might be tempted to ask if there's something supernatural about it, something magical. Or is it perhaps simply the eternal beauty that is so sublime it hurts?

'In Surabaya I met a man who had withdrawn from the world and left his position, his family, and his future, and who spent his time building a temple in the Egyptian style. It was dedicated to Nefertiti, and he planned to live there. Her casts stood everywhere, and a famous painter had, at his request, painted her portrait which hung above the altar. And in Saigon, I heard about a young man who travelled to Germany to study; he was supposed to become something as prosaic as a businessman, a level-headed lad, a sportsman, or a lightweight local politician. But in Berlin, one day, he saw Nefertiti. From that day, he abandoned his studies and spent his days in the museum. He arrived early in the morning and didn't leave until closing time. When he finally returned to Saigon, he shot himself.

'Her following is everywhere – explain it, whoever can – call it reincarnation, echoes of a former existence that suddenly stirs within us at the sight of this masterpiece … In Ancient Egypt, two cities fought a war for years over the queen's bust, and modern Egypt has lodged an official protest in Berlin demanding its return … A following indeed! In Engadin, I met a monk; in Iowa, a millionaire with horn–rimmed glasses. He was dismayed when he learned that the bust was not for sale.'

Winterstein had become quite eloquent, his voice no longer harsh and unsympathetic; the man seemed entirely changed, filled with life and warmth.

'Do you know,' he continued, 'that the museum's management still receives requests from people wishing to spend a night in the museum, among the ancient and eerie Egyptian artefacts, in the room where the bust is displayed? Yes, you may smile, but there are people who become entirely entranced by such a passion.'

'Have you seen her?' he asked suddenly, turning to Anne Marie.

She shook her head.

'Imagine a dimly lit room, like an Egyptian tomb. If you've come straight in from outside, you can't immediately see anything, except one thing in the centre of the room. It's the bust, standing in a spotlight. She wears the blue headpiece of the Egyptian queens, with the sacred uraeus ornament, the symbol of gods and kings. And then you see her … Her brown face emerges in the light … The high and boldly arched eyebrows, the fine and wonderfully sensitive features, a straight nose, a subtly ironic and perhaps slightly weary smile around the full, living, sensual mouth. As though she is a little tired of the millennia, but nonetheless receives mankind's homage with a secret joy, because she is divine and the most beautiful and perfect woman who has ever lived. This must also be what Cleopatra looked like – so beautiful, so wise, so alive – and so full of disdain for the world …'

He suddenly drained his glass and continued with growing intensity, addressing Anne Marie:

'And if you stand there for a while in front of her, you'll also notice one of her eyes, the left, is damaged. At first, her gaze is cold and hard; the technique, the glaze, perhaps wasn't quite perfected at the time, one might think,' – he glanced at me – 'though wrongly so, but then suddenly you feel that she's looking at you. You'll sense that she's speaking to you alone in the whole world. A spark of life leaps forth, a secret bond between you ... But ... Then it's not just you but a congregation, a following ... That's the tragic part.

'When you look around the room, you discover other people in the half–light, and they drift about, make small loops to and fro, pause at other busts, tear themselves away, and head towards the exit, only to return! There you have Nefertiti's congregation; those whose Mecca is this very room, and who long to return there wherever they may be in the world ... Forgive me,' he said suddenly, 'I forgot myself – I've clearly spoken too much – I beg your pardon. May I just express my admiration for your excellent taste,' he added, turning to me.

He fell silent, as one does when one has said too much and regrets it. We remained at the table a while longer. Winterstein didn't touch his glass again, but Adrian drank steadily and grew cheerfully and blissfully relaxed. He could do with it. We moved out onto the veranda. Winterstein looked at the view and got his bearings.

'So that is Hasselbakken,' he said, pronouncing it awkwardly and with difficulty; he clearly thought it was a damnable word to wrestle with.

A violet dusk had slowly settled over the countryside. The landscape lay waiting for a release from the heavens; dark, heavy clouds loomed in the distance. No birds sang anymore, no grasshoppers 'sawed'; nature was silent.

'When did you first meet my husband?' asked Anne Marie suddenly, turning to Winterstein.

'We met relatively late,' he answered. 'The war was practically over.'

'But I thought you were war comrades?'

'You become that, in a way,' muttered Adrian.

'We made the retreat together,' explained Winterstein.

'Were you also with the staff?' I asked, just to keep the topic alive.

'No,' answered Winterstein, 'I was a military railway commander over three small front stations in Podolia – Kasatin, Rushin and Daudsewas – it was at the last station that I met – he hesitated slightly – 'Adrian Krebs, for the first time.'

'Tell us,' suggested Anne Marie. 'You spoke so vividly about the Egyptian queen; we'd like to hear more.'

'It's a different sort of story,' said Winterstein darkly; it was clear that he was reluctant to give in to our persuasion. I supported Anne Marie; Adrian said nothing.

'Well then,' said Winterstein, 'it was in early December 1918, I don't remember the exact date anymore. The war was officially over, but tattered remnants of German and Austrian troops were still deep inside Russia. Everything was in disarray, no Field Marshal von Hindenburg had taken charge on our front and made sure the troops were brought home. The staff had abandoned us, the large formations had already been withdrawn across the border, while small outposts and units in many places were simply forgotten and left to themselves, without orders, without supplies, and in many cases with insufficient weapons and ammunition. The countryside was in full revolt.

'Petlyura, the Ukrainian military commander, was trying to govern from Kiev with his Cossacks, but in Kamianets–Podilskyi, a workers' and soldiers' council was in control and refused to recognise him; in the north, Polish irregulars stood their ground.

The situation changed from day to day, there was nothing firm to hold on to; rumours flew and were usually unreliable. Red soldiers roamed around fighting; now and then the villagers revolted against our soldiers and killed them. Even proper bandit gangs were at large; it was chaos, and each man had to fend for himself.

'Small groups of our soldiers banded together and tried to fight their way westward; they longed to be home for Christmas. They fought, marched, rode, drove; occasionally they used the railway for short stretches, but always with the utmost caution. The next town could be in enemy hands, the front was everywhere and on all sides; it was civil war, and we were all outlaws. And tired … Tired to death after four years of war …'

He paused before continuing:

'I had, as mentioned, command of three small front–line stations, and the corps' orders were that they were to be held until the rearguard's commander informed me that I could join the retreat. But other dispositions must have been made – the rearguard perhaps took another route, or was annihilated – I never heard anything from them. I sat there waiting in Kasatin, which was the westernmost station, and therefore closest to home. It was a small town of a few thousand people; filthy, muddy, dreadful.

'But nothing happened. Two days passed with no movement on the line; no trains came, no troops passed by, and the telephone line was cut. For the defence of the entire line, I had six men, and a few train personnel in Kasatin. Something had to happen at any moment. I waited and waited. Eventually, I decided to take the handcar eastwards. I brought along my clerk, Schneckenburger. After a couple of hours of riding, we reached Rushin, my second station; not a soul in sight. The station had been looted and the guard had disappeared, perhaps killed? Murdered? A couple of men claimed he had joined some soldiers passing through. It was impossible to investigate further. In a gloomy mood, we continued to Daudsewas.

'Daudsewas is the most godforsaken hole imaginable; a shack in the middle of a small plain, lying in a hollow and surrounded by bare, muddy, cheerless hills. Not a living soul in sight nearby; the nearest village lies three versts away. A road crosses the railway line, which is the only reason the station had been built. I once spent three weeks there while the stationmaster was ill; three weeks of complete isolation, apart from swarms of flies that made life hell day and night.

'Lying carelessly up on the slope is a rusted water tank, glowing red as a reminder of the Russian demolitions when they abandoned Daudsewas. That was the first thing we saw. The next was Boehm, the stationmaster, sitting on a pile of planks, smoking a pipe. "Thank God," he said, "I had started wondering whether everyone in the world was dead; nothing has happened here for the past three days, not a soul has come by." He invited us in and lit the stove, a round iron container that soon glowed red–hot. Then he laid the table with cups and pewter plates and set a bottle of beer on the table, his last one.

'I remember the menu clearly, our last meal in Daudsewas; it consisted of an enormous slice of bread per man. Instead of butter, the slice was covered with fried blood sausage, smeared on in thick layers. The host made no apology for the fare; it was entirely acceptable. Had he done so, it would surely have been meant as a joke; none of us were used to anything better. We ate in silence and enjoyed the warmth; only the swarms of flies disturbed us. When we reached out, we caught a handful each time. To get rid of them, we tossed them into the red–hot stove. In clouds, they circled above our bread. We cursed and ate; flies, blood sausage, and soldier's stump. It tasted wonderful; outside it was freezing.

'Then suddenly we froze where we sat around the primitive table; there were voices outside. Schneckenburger reached for his carbine, Boehm and I were armed with pistols; such were the times. We had been careless and allowed ourselves to be surprised. But it turned out to be four German Landsturm soldiers; bearded, dirty, and exhausted. There was still a little bread and sausage left for them. They came from the east and hadn't seen any other German troops. They believed they were the last …

'It was clear to me that I could no longer guard my three stations. I had simply been forgotten; I had to act on my own.

'We held a council. One of the Landsturm men had a map. As transport, we had the handcar. The seven of us agreed to stick together. It was late in the afternoon, and we decided to spend the night in the station building, as best we could. We ate the rest of our provisions. One of the Landsturm men sang a little; he was from Swabia. He sang some melancholic folk songs that brought tears of homesickness to our eyes.

'Later that evening, we noticed a red glow on the horizon to the west, in the direction of Kasatin. There could be no doubt; the town was on fire. We could also faintly hear the crackle of machine guns when the wind carried the sound. We posted a guard to avoid being surprised in our sleep. In the middle of the night, two more joined us; it was Krebs and Soten. They had horses, small, scruffy, shaggy Cossack ponies; God knows where they had got them from. Soten also wore a large Russian soldier's coat; it was better than our own threadbare ones.

'They came riding along the road and were challenged by our sentry as they approached the line. The rest of us were alarmed and turned out. When we heard the reason, we cursed our lost sleep but were glad for the reinforcements. There were nine of us the next morning.'

Adrian nodded to himself.

Winterstein continued:

'We had decided to set out early the next morning and had planned to travel in a wide arc northward around Kasatin. We made the final preparations and destroyed the station's documents. We were already ready to depart when Boehm suddenly put his ear to the tracks and said he heard something rolling. We couldn't see far down the line; it made a sharp bend between clay hills.

'We stood uncertainly for a moment, then we spread out and prepared to fire. Eventually, a railway wagon appeared, an open freight car being slowly pushed forward by three men. A red flag was fastened to the front of the wagon. The three faltered when they saw us. Then they waved and shouted a hesitant "Kamerad". One of them was a Russian soldier, wearing a uniform with a red armband. The other two were civilians, though partly clad in military gear; one wore a cape, the other an old–type German soldier's helmet with a spike on top.

'They were as dirty and bearded as we were. "Perhaps we can ask for news," said Soten, putting down his rifle, "the rest of you stay here and cover me." He shoved both hands in his trouser pockets and walked towards them. That was his way, reckless and indifferent; he had several medals for bravery. It took a while before he came back, a cigarette in his mouth. "They'd like to come into the station and cook a bit of food," he said, "we might as well agree to it." We nodded; better to try kindness. Soten shouted something across in Russian.

'But the three clearly took no chances; it took a while before they came. They conferred animatedly, then two of them emerged. The third stayed behind; we could see his rifle barrel sticking up behind some crates loaded onto the railway wagon. The two came forward with caution and watched us closely. They had carbines slung over their shoulders, revolver grips sticking out of their pockets, and three–handled grenades dangling from their belts. These were men who could fight back. Their mistrust rubbed off on us; we withdrew slightly and kept an eye on them. A couple of the Landsturm men whistled the Internationale; the two strangers didn't seem to hear it.

'Soten wandered about on his own without a rifle; I saw him up on the hillside. A little later, he came back down to us, agitated. He asked us to withdraw a bit; he had something on his mind. "Do you know what they have on the wagon?" he whispered, "a machine gun with ammunition; a German machine gun!"

'We didn't understand at first. "Don't you get it,' he continued, 'that if it were ours, our chances of breaking through would increase enormously; a machine gun is worth fifty men. It would give us tremendous firepower." We were still uncertain. Soten moved again towards the wagon and disappeared behind it. After a while, he returned. "One of them says they're forced to push the wagon because of the heavy load,", gesturing back over his shoulder. "And he says that if only they had a couple of horses …"

'He paused. Then he whispered hoarsely: "I think they're planning to take our horses from us."

'"We outnumber them," one of the Landsturm men objected.

'"A hand grenade is enough to finish you all as you're standing here," replied Soten contemptuously.

'"But we could take their machine gun …"

'To make a long story short, Soten got his way. He pointed out that it was a German machine gun, spoils of war; it was just a matter of reclaiming it. "I'll take care of it," he said with an ominous smile, "if only someone could join me. And let me borrow a pistol; I'll keep it in my pocket. I'm left–handed and shoot left; they won't expect that."

'He got my big Parabellum. A Landsturm man named Mendel went with him. Meanwhile, the Russian who had stayed behind to guard the wagon appeared and asked for matches. We tossed a box over to him; he picked it up and withdrew again … At that very moment, shots rang out from inside the cabin. A windowpane shattered; we heard a couple of screams, then everything fell silent …

'The fellow with the matches took to his heels. "Shoot!" someone among us shouted; I had no weapon, Soten had mine, but someone, I think it was St … Adrian fired …

'No,' said Adrian loudly, 'I have never killed a man—'

'Well then, it must have been Krauter who fired,' continued Winterstein indifferently, 'the Russian threw up his arms like one does when shot through the heart, and fell heavily into the mud.. The machine gun was ours, but Mendel had taken a bullet through the shoulder. Do you remember that; wasn't that how it happened?' Winterstein turned towards Adrian.

Adrian nodded.

'Did Soten shoot down the two other Russians immediately?' I asked.

'I don't think so,' said Winterstein, 'they parleyed for a while, as far as I remember from Soten's account afterward. The Russians wanted us to join them, and when that didn't work, they demanded our horses. They said, as I recall, that they could pepper us with their machine gun and that they had reinforcements nearby. It was fair play, both parties were prepared; but Soten had the advantage of speed, he could shoot from his pocket and left–handed.'

'You were part of this, Adrian?' asked Anne Marie.

'Otherwise, your husband wouldn't be sitting here, madam,' answered Winterstein coldly. 'That's how the times were; it was their lives or ours. We were surrounded by death and disaster on all sides, and only the hardest survived.'

'So the Russians were Bolsheviks?' I asked.

'I don't know,' said Winterstein, 'at least they had a red flag with them. Our clash had nothing to do with politics; I believe most of us were fairly red ourselves back then. They wanted our horses, we wanted their machine gun, that was all.'

'Yes, that's how we were brought together,' mumbled Adrian.

'And then?' I asked.

'We moved on immediately. Mendel, who was wounded, was placed on one horse, the machine gun and some ammunition on the other. We filled our pockets and knapsacks with the precious ammunition …'

He paused; a faint rumbling vibrated through the air. It was distant thunder, a storm approaching in the gloom.

Suddenly Winterstein pointed out into the darkness and asked sharply: 'There; is that your house?'

Adrian followed his finger. 'Yes,' he said, 'that's Hasselbakken.'

Winterstein got to his feet. 'There was a light,' he said calmly. 'A light came on upstairs.'

'The maid—?' I asked Anne Marie.

'She's in her own home,' she answered curtly, 'I only have a day maid.'

'Good God, a break–in! Call the police, Adrian!'

At that moment, the telephone rang. Adrian, who was nearest, picked it up. He turned around with the receiver in hand, and his voice was trembling. 'The girl at the telephone exchange says that an alarm bell is ringing continuously!'

'Well,' said Winterstein calmly, 'then call Falk at once and tell him.'

Adrian asked for the hotel's number. Winterstein stood beside him, dictating to him word by word.

'Yes, this is Krebs, Adrian Krebs; the alarm bell is ringing like mad.'

'No, we're not home, we're over at Wiig's.'

'Yes, we'll head over at once.'

'How long?'

Adrian turned to me. 'Ten minutes,' I whispered.

Adrian didn't hear but stared absentmindedly into space and repeated the question angrily. I held up ten fingers to make him understand.

'We can be there in ten minutes,' he said into the phone.

'Tell him to carry out everything as agreed,' said Winterstein.

Adrian did so with a trembling voice; the hand holding the receiver was shaking.

Winterstein remained completely calm. 'Right, let's head over there,' he said coolly, as though it were a perfectly ordinary evening stroll. 'Perhaps you and Mrs Krebs should stay behind,' he said to me.

'No,' said Anne Marie firmly. 'I'm coming too; I want to know what's happening in my own house.'

'I'm coming too,' I said.

'Then you should bring that revolver you mentioned yesterday,' said Winterstein dryly, 'and remember, it's an advantage to shoot left–handed.'

He laughed with his low, unpleasant laugh.

We left. The wind had started howling in the trees and drowned out all other sound. A few large, heavy raindrops fell but stopped again quickly. It was as dark as it can be on an autumn evening. Winterstein walked ahead, then the rest of us followed. From time to time, he turned around to ask the way.

Halfway up the hill, we were stopped, Adrian stepped forward. 'All clear?' he asked quietly.

'No one has come this way,' answered a man's voice from the shadow of a spruce.

'Then they must still be there,' mumbled Winterstein. 'Go on, tell the men that they can join us.'

Two figures emerged from the woods and followed us. We continued walking. The revolver was heavy in my pocket.

'Is anyone here?' one of the strangers suddenly shouted. We had reached the house.

Winterstein hushed him and gave instructions to Adrian, who let them go on ahead. The two newcomers were placed behind the house, while the rest of us approached the veranda door. I asked Anne Marie to stay back, but she didn't respond. Adrian unlocked the door; it took a moment before he found the keyhole. Winterstein said something in a sharp tone.

We thoroughly searched the ground floor and lit lights everywhere. Before we went upstairs, Winterstein went down into the cellar; there were no signs of intruders. Then we began climbing to the upper floor. Winterstein was still in charge. We searched all the rooms and finally came to the veranda room. Winterstein knocked. No answer. He rattled the door. It was locked.

Winterstein took out the key and looked around. He was calm and deliberate, and didn't rush. First, he made sure to turn off the light. Then he asked us to stand aside. I noticed he held the key in his left hand and kept close to the wall. Then came a click; the door was open. A second later, the room was lit.

It was empty!

It was immediately apparent that an intruder had been there. The veranda door had been opened from the outside, a piece of the windowpane cut out, and someone had simply reached in and turned the key. The thief, or thieves, must have simply climbed up onto the veranda to get in.

'Is anything stolen?' asked Anne Marie.

Winterstein didn't answer; something barbarically triumphant had come over his face. We followed his gaze.

In the corner on a table stood a metre–high, richly ornate panel, inlaid with mother–of–pearl, gold, and ebony. Three artfully crafted figures of pure gold symbolised the Holy Trinity; it was a masterpiece. With half a glance, I could see it was a unique rarity. It was fixed to the wall by a steel chain.

Winterstein went over to the panel; his face had retained its expression, but now it also shone with anticipation. He laid his hand lightly on the dove symbolising the Holy Spirit; there was a faint click, the front of the panel opened, and a painting came into view; a marvellous Madonna figure painted in blue, in every shade from the darkest to the lightest, most jubilant sky blue. An intense light radiated from the painting, and involuntarily I closed my eyes; then I heard another click, and the panel had closed again.

We all stood in silence.

'Madonna awaiting the child,' said Winterstein quietly, almost tenderly.

There was movement by the door. A slight, fair–haired man had entered in a long grey raincoat wet across the shoulders; the storm had begun. Winterstein shook his hand.

'All in order,' said the man in the raincoat, 'I've phoned, our people are in place, and the police have been informed.'

'Excellent, Herr Falk,' said Winterstein, rubbing his hands, 'things are going splendidly. The thieves have clearly been frightened off,' he added with a peculiar and unpleasant smile.

The two men who had joined us on the road came up the stairs; they had something to report. One had found a footprint; he spoke excitedly and insisted that it had to be preserved and a casting made immediately before the rain washed it away.

Falk stood hesitantly, weighing the matter. Winterstein's voice cut in, as he grasped the topic.

'There's no need,' he said to Falk. 'What use is a footprint when we have photographs of the culprits?'

'So the system worked?' asked Falk, interested.

'Yes,' said Winterstein, 'the film is wound, and all 36 exposures were taken.'

'I'm pleased,' said Falk, elated. 'It's actually the first time I've had the chance to work with something like this; I had no personal experience and had to rely on the engineer.'

Winterstein met my eyes; his satisfaction was no less than the young Falk's. He paused for a moment, then gave in to the temptation to explain:

'You see the chain,' he said, 'it was nothing really; practically there just for show. But here, you see this device—' he pointed to a black, oblong box, '—here you have one of the most ingenious protective measures modern technology has produced. It's supposedly quite expensive, but a marvellous invention. Have you heard of infrared rays?'

He waited a little, glancing about before continuing:

'Well, between this device and a contact in the wall directly opposite, I can, when leaving the room, establish a continuous stream of invisible rays. Anyone trying to reach my painting must break this stream; but he has no idea he's done so, it's completely imperceptible. Naturally, this break in the current can be used in various ways. It can be linked to an alarm system, that's the most common, or it can trigger a camera. This construction did both. The moment the current was broken, an alarm rang throughout the house, but as we weren't present, I had arranged for the alarm to be transmitted via the telephone network to the exchange, which then rang us. As you'll remember, the call came as soon as we saw the light at the house. Can you guess why the thieves turned on the light?'

I shook my head.

'Because the camera whirred ever so softly during the exposure. Naturally, the culprits had an electric torch with them, but when they heard that unexplained sound in the dark, they panicked and switched on the light at once. They felt they'd been outsmarted, gave up their attempt, and fled.'

'Then that's a flaw,' said Falk thoughtfully, 'that sound must be removed next time.'

'On the contrary,' said Winterstein slowly, musing, 'perhaps it was just as well the thieves were frightened off.'

CHAPTER VI

This incident consumed me; there were things about it that I could not understand, circumstances which seemed to directly contradict one another. But I consoled myself with the thought that the solution was imminent; a state of high tension had been reached, and the resolution had to be near. Within 24 hours we ought to expect important events; Winterstein's triumphant attitude had told me that.

And then absolutely nothing happened. That is to say, the mortal enemies, who 'would chase each other to death,' reconciled!

Adrian came over towards noon; he was in good spirits and almost like his old self. He said that Winterstein and Falk had gone into Oslo. They had just telephoned; Winterstein would return on an afternoon train and was bringing guests with him. Would I also like to come over for supper?

'It's been a hellish time for me,' he added, 'but now it's over.'

'I've understood that you've had it tough', I said.

'One day, when they have left, you'll get the whole story,' said Adrian.

'What does Anne Marie say about last night's incident?'

'Strangely, nothing at all,' said Adrian. 'She probably thinks it was an ordinary burglary,' he added hopefully.

I thought to myself that he was gravely underestimating his wife; the alarm system, infrared beams, the Madonna painting … Anne Marie's thoughtful silence throughout the entire incident last night … I was curious to hear what she would say when I saw her again, and a little afraid of what she might ask me.

'When shall I come this evening?' I asked, still following that train of thought. 'By the way, who are the guests?'

'Soten and Jan,' answered Adrian lightly.

'The burglars from last night?' I said, astonished. 'And today you let them into your house? I don't understand anything anymore.'

'It may look a bit strange,' Adrian admitted, 'but the thing is we're old war comrades – that binds us, inevitably – and we've made peace and come to an arrangement. Come over around seven; I'll tell them not to mention Heilige Lampe.'

I arrived before the guests. There was one train per hour, and theirs had been delayed. Adrian was upstairs getting dressed, and Anne Marie received me alone.

'What do you think about what happened last night?' she asked immediately.

'I don't know what to believe,' I answered truthfully.

'A strange man arrives and takes up lodging in our home,' she continued, agitated, 'and immediately arranges for a break–in. He installs electrical warning devices and places guards around the house, yet he himself goes away on the very night something happens. And he doesn't seem afraid …'

'No,' I admitted.

'And the thieves, go about it in an utterly idiotic way. At midnight, they climb up the veranda posts in a way that would have woken the whole house, had we been at home. We can assume that they must have known no one was home; they have all the time in the world. Yet they let themselves be scared off by a faint whirring sound in the room. Can you understand any of this?'

'No,' I said. 'I've also thought about why the thieves didn't simply cut out the panel if it was the painting they were after.'

'Maybe they didn't know how to open it,' said Anne Marie thoughtfully, 'and it was probably too much trouble to take the entire thing with them.'

Anne Marie was wearing a simple white dress.

'You look marvellous today,' I said.

'You know we're having guests,' she smiled. 'Two interesting guests, Adrian's war comrades suddenly showed up. Do you remember our conversation in the spring, when I complained that nothing ever happened? Well, I'm not complaining now; but I do hope I'll learn more before the evening is over.'

'What will you do?' I asked.

' I'll take action,' she said. 'There's something behind all this, and I want to get to the bottom of it.'

'But how?'

'I'll try to learn more about what happened back then; I want to know what became of Adrian and his eight comrades after they left Dau … that station, what was it called again?'

'Daudsewas,' I said. 'Daudsewas in Podolia.'

―

Anne Marie was a radiant hostess that evening, the only lady present and the centre of attention. She was in excellent, almost exuberant spirits, and united us all in pleasant harmony . The two strangers, Soten and Jan – he was introduced, but I didn't catch his surname, which contained an overwhelming number of consonants – conducted themselves most amiably. Cultivated and knowledgeable men, they easily adapted to the setting and were both exquisitely attentive towards Anne Marie. For her part, she made it clear that she appreciated the international character of the gathering, and she drew out from Jan that he was Polish, while Winterstein and Soten were Germans. She also managed, as only a woman can, to swiftly find out how Soten and Jan had spent the years after the war.

Both had been swept up in the great cauldron of the East and Asia, the endless, years–long civil wars and upheavals sprawling across the continent's vastness. 'People in this country don't even recognise the names of the conflicts,' said Soten with a quiet smile to himself. His fate had led him to the White factions across the Russian continent; for a time he had served as an officer under the Turkish revolutionary Enver Pasha, but he 'unfortunately' was absent the night Enver was ambushed and killed somewhere in Bokhara, in the Uzbek Soviet Republic.

Later came names like Zhang Zuolin, Wu Peifu, and expeditions and skirmishes near Manchurian and Mongolian towns; names we barely knew even from the newswires. Indeed, we didn't recognise them at all. The same blind and arbitrary fate had carried his comrade Jan away, but on the opposite side. He had followed the Reds and had also served as an officer. He had served under Soviet commanders like Brusilov, Blyukher, and Budyonny. Barbaric images were conjured before us: we sensed death marches through deserts, months–long battles of bitter intensity, bloody atrocities, the massacres of towns and villages. Suffering, death, horror.

And now they sat there speaking of it as if it had been a normal day at work. Such was the way of the world several thousand miles away. They had, so to speak, merely stepped out of that world for a while; and now they could relax and enjoy the luxuries of civilisation for a time. They were polite, well–mannered, and had kissed the hostess's hand when they arrived. Tall and upright, muscular and carefree, they were men used to claiming their place in life …

I sat for a while, lost in my own thoughts.

'I'm truly among adventurers this evening,' said Anne Marie suddenly, turning to me.

'No, among mercenaries,' corrected Soten. 'If you need us, madam, we are at your service.'

His tone was light and playful, but his eyes were serious, and around his mouth there was the hint of a wolfish grin. I was suddenly struck with an intense sense of unease. Anne Marie flattered the two men, but I knew where she was heading and did not feel left out. Yet I could not rid myself of the feeling that something sinister threatened us all; it descended like a black shadow upon me. Anne Marie resumed the conversation after dinner. I got the impression that both Winterstein and Adrian tried in vain to divert her, but she would not be dissuaded.

'I heard your name for the first time yesterday,' she said to Soten. 'Isn't it strange, considering that you and my husband are old war comrades?'

'We never speak of the past,' interjected Adrian quickly.

'May I ask in what context my name was mentioned?' asked Soten politely.

'It was in connection with a small front–line station and a machine gun. The station was called Daudsewas. You captured a machine gun.'

'I see,' said Soten, thoughtfully. 'Yes, I vaguely recall something of the sort.'

Soten sat there and truly did not remember that he had killed two men it merely 'vaguely occurred' to him. 'Yes, I suppose that's right,' he said after a moment. 'One of my comrades fell in the same incident. What was his name again …? So much has happened since then,' he added.

'Mendel,' said Winterstein shortly.

Anne Marie pressed on. 'We got just that far last night, but then we were interrupted by a burglary. Did you know that our house was broken into last night?'

'I've heard so,' said Soten calmly.

Adrian began speaking loudly about something else, but no one paid him any attention, and Winterstein reached for the cigar box and offered it around on the host's behalf. Soten smiled faintly, and Jan, too, had become visibly interested. Both were probably captivated by Anne Marie. Thanks to her, they had taken centre stage at dinner; perhaps naturally so. They were Adrian's old comrades who had suddenly turned up. Yes, it was perfectly in order.

'I would really like to know what happened after you left Daudsewas,' said Anne Marie coaxingly. 'Adrian has never told me anything about it. He never wants to speak of these things; it's all completely new to me.'

'Anne Marie,' said Adrian in distress, 'you're just troubling our guests.'

He had addressed her in Norwegian – otherwise, the conversation had been in German – but it was as if Jan had guessed the nature of his words. His gaze passed between them and he suddenly said aloud:

'But why not? Why not dwell once more on what happened, now when we can tell our story to a young, beautiful woman? Let's hear her opinion on our actions before we cast the past aside. Let's summon the dead.'

His voice sounded hollow and distant, like a chant; it was as much an invocation to the past and its dead as to us. The riders of the Apocalypse had gathered, and the ghosts of the past rose once more under their thundering hooves.

Outside, the sky was leaden black; rain fell in torrents. A blinding white flash tore through the air and lit up the room, revealing our pale faces; then the thunder crashed, as though the very vault of heaven had been rent apart above our heads. The lights went out.

'Do as the young lady wishes,' Jan told Soten. 'Tell us about the ride to Olesko; I believe you recall it best.'

Soten rubbed his forehead as though trying to wipe away the intervening years; he was clearly trying to remember, and he began slowly and hesitantly:

'No, I was wrong. Mendel didn't fall at Daudsewas; he was only wounded there. He didn't die until Olesko. There were nine of us when we left the station that morning: three railway soldiers and four Landwehr men, then there was … our host and myself.'

'We had two horses and, of course, the machine gun. We headed north the next day, avoiding the danger in Kasatin, where we could see the smoke on the horizon. We abandoned the road and crossed fields and meadows. The weather had grown milder, and there was a bit of rain; the ground was soft and marshy. We sank in up to our ankles. Mendel, who was wounded, rode. We reached a village by evening, and a couple of the men dared to go in and managed to buy food for a few days. We had a little money and, besides that, cartridges. We didn't dare stay in the village overnight; we were too few. Instead we settled in a sparse wood some distance away, but didn't dare light a fire, for fear that the villagers would discover us. We froze bitterly; it was worst for Mendel.

'For several days we continued, I don't remember much more precisely; it hardly matters. None of us spoke much. We didn't know each other and didn't know what the other was worth; we only knew that we were seeing each other from our worst side, and that we were all at rock bottom. It was sheer necessity that kept us together. A couple of the Landsturm men passed the time cursing the Kaiser, the government and the officers, but they soon stopped when no one contradicted them.

'We dragged ourselves forward in a daze. Each one of us brooded over a single thought: What now? What will become of us when we return home to defeat and continued misery? Who has the means to get by? Wouldn't it be just as well to end up here in a common grave? That was the mood we were in. We were broken, finished, no longer soldiers. We were a band, like all the others, and only now and then did something flash through us; that explains what later happened. .One day we were fired upon from the edge of a forest; another day, church bells rang as we passed through a village, calling the villagers to arms. We veered north, always north and away from the course we should have kept.

'One rainy day we followed a ravine; I was in the lead. When I reached the top of the slope, I spotted twenty or thirty horsemen a few kilometres away. They were travelling in the same direction as us, but diagonally. We might be able to get them within shooting range. From their pointed hats, we could tell they were Cossacks. That meant a lot to us; it meant horses. With horses, our chances would improve. We were exhausted from stumbling through the mud. We brought the machine gun into position and prepared to fire. One of us prayed to God that the riders would come closer; a couple of others swore; maybe it balanced out. Mendel groaned.

'But suddenly the riders changed course and our chance vanished. Schneckenburger started mouthing off; I floored him into the mud. He got back up, and we went on. I made sure not to turn my back on him. We continued along the ravine. A couple of hours later, we saw a cluster of houses in the distance; the Cossacks had dismounted, and the horses stood tied outside. We got the machine gun into position, compared watches and agreed on the time; four of us crept towards the rear of the house, two stayed ready to seize the horses, and three remained at the machine gun.

'Having arrived, we fired a few shots at the roof. The Cossacks rushed out and ran straight into our trap. They took cover on the opposite side of the house and returned fire. Then we had them. The machine gun gave them one long and two short bursts, and it was over. We got the horses, one each and four spare; the rest had been hit. Things moved more quickly now that we had horses, and we could veer south again, where settlements were dense. But we didn't dare go indoors.

'The weather had turned colder; the ground froze. After a while, the horses started to suffer from being out night after night. We gave up; we couldn't be bothered anymore. We didn't even fear a mass grave –we didn't care about anything – and rode into Olesko on the thirteenth of December. We heard there was a gentleman who kept an inn somewhere in the village. He first said he had no room, but that was a lie, and all nine of us settled in. We also found a stable for the horses nearby. It was a blessing to get a roof over our heads. We were filthy and bearded and hadn't taken off our uniforms in weeks. We were all lice–ridden.'

He fell silent. We waited. It was clear he had no intention of saying more. Another crash of thunder shook the windows.

Anne Marie looked at Jan. 'But you,' she said, 'weren't you part of this? You haven't been mentioned.'

'No,' said Jan slowly, 'I wasn't part of the ride from Daudsewas to Olesko. I joined them later.'

Winterstein interrupted: 'If this charade is to continue, I too must reserve the right to speak. In any case, I believe it would be best for all of us to let the past remain buried.'

'What purpose does it serve to rake it all up again? Times were completely different back then; if we were to meet ourselves as we were then, we'd be facing strangers.'

Jan looked at him for a long time; another flash of lightning cut across the room and was reflected in his staring eyes.

'You've had your way,' he said with finality, 'now let us have ours.' The thunderclap made the house shake; outside it was pitch dark, and a few candles that Anne Marie had placed in candlesticks cast a flickering glow. Now and then they nearly went out; the wind howled, and draughts came in from the open windows. All the forces of heaven and earth were on the move tonight.

Adrian had slumped into a sofa and said nothing, his face pale blue–white and ghostly. 'No, I wasn't there,' Jan repeated slowly, 'I wasn't a soldier, I was a monk. Somewhere inside White Russia lies a town called Borodjanka; it's been renamed now. I had lived there for three years; I was to take my monastic vows in seven months' time.

'Our monastery possessed a precious, famous, miraculous image: the Madonna Expecting the Child; or the Blue Madonna, as the image was also called because of its colouring. We knew the history of the painting and knew that it had the power to heal. On three occasions in history, it had even raised the dead; the last time was a generation ago. Thousands came to our monastery every year, and thousands brought offerings; our monastery was especially sought out by expectant mothers or by women who could not conceive. We naturally loved this image; it was our greatest treasure and had, for centuries, brought our monastery its renown and fame. One day, the prior of the monastery came to me in my cell.

'"My son," he said, "I must lay upon you a great responsibility, a heavy burden, but also a great honour. The Antichrist is ravaging the world; at any moment our monastery may fall, and robbers' hands may add to our Madonna's martyrdom. I know only one place that has always withstood the attacks of the ungodly, namely Jasna Góra in Częstochowa, in Poland. You are the only Pole among us; you know the language and will be able to make your way. Moreover, you are from a Polish noble family, and your pure heart assures me that you will fulfil this task despite your youth."'

He paused. Once again, the thunder rolled over our heads. Three, four violent flashes followed in quick succession, and then a great crash; it must have struck nearby.

'He said those words; he said your pure heart …' Jan's voice, for a moment, was filled with pain and bitter scorn. Then he continued:

'"No one would suspect a poor monk of carrying anything precious and sacred," the prior continued. "I know no other way. In the monastery at Jasna Góra live our brethren ; they belong to the Pauline order, at least in name, although they are Roman Catholic. They will not deny us refuge. Time and again, heathens have tried to storm the walls of the monastery. The Turks tried, and the Swedes, but the Mother of God in Częstochowa appeared in white over the walls and struck fear and horror into the soldiers."

'I should take our Madonna to her holy sister; to the Matka Boska Częstochowska, the Black Madonna . So the prior told me, and had me swear on the cross. I lay down and prayed to be given strength to carry out my mission, and I prayed for forgiveness for letting my unworthy hands touch our miraculous Madonna. Then the prior lit a torch, and we entered the holy chapel in the middle of the night. We both fell to our knees before her and begged forgiveness for our sins and for taking her away; but we also knew that if she disapproved, no power on earth would be able to move her from that place.

'We removed the entire icon, and I was also given a pouch containing some of the jewels she had received as offerings through the ages; it was a treasure in itself. I hid the pouch against my chest, but I couldn't carry the painting, and we were afraid to use a horse or a donkey, in case it was taken from me. Then we found the solution: I took the monastery's light handcart and had a dog harnessed to it. No one would take that pitiful vehicle from me. And so I left my holy monastery like a thief in the night. I have never seen it again; it was pillaged and burned shortly afterwards.'

He paused again and waited. Outside the thunder had stopped; but the rain still poured down. Jan's voice sounded weary as he continued:

'You're unfamiliar with our holy church, so you don't know Poland's great sanctuary at Jasna Góra. A million people make pilgrimage there every year to seek strength and comfort from the famous Black Madonna. She is called that because of the image's dark and sombre colouring; she doesn't have the heavenly glow of our Madonna. The image, painted by the evangelist Luke, was brought to Poland five hundred years ago; we know its whole history. And the Pauline monks, through all these years, have given their lives for their holy treasure, and their Madonna has smiled upon them and protected them.

'Once, daring robbers attempted to steal the sacred image, and in their arrogance, one of them struck the face of the Mother of God twice with a sabre. Then lightning struck the altar and killed the blasphemer. The marks are still visible today, although renowned artists have tried to cover them. But they reappear again and again; not as gashes in the wood, but as scars on her face. She wanted them to remain, to remind mankind of human shame and awaken them to prayer and repentance.

'Częstochowa is the town with the monastery. It is to this day what it has always been: Poland's holy city with the famous Black Madonna. To her I was to bring our monastery's image and save it from destruction. No one noticed a poor monk, a dog, and a rickety cart, though I was mocked by godless people wherever I went. But sometimes I met devout folk who helped me.

'For twenty days I travelled westward. A couple of times there was fighting ahead of me, and I had to take detours. On the twenty–first day, late in the evening, I reached Olesko, tired and hungry. I can still see the last stretch of road into the village before me: the fields lay blue–white with frost in the darkness, the trees stretched their bare frozen branches toward the cloudy sky, and snow drifted through the air. There was not a soul in sight, silence lay all around; I was so utterly alone. And yet Satan and my evil fate strode beside me on the slippery, icy road; it was the thirteenth of December, autumn 1918.

'I knocked on a cottage door but found no lodging. I went from door to door, but no one would take in a poor monk; people's hearts were hard. Somewhere I was told to try the inn run by Ephraim. It was a malicious, mocking voice that told me this; I was young and thought nothing of it. I stumbled on through the uneven, frozen streets, my dog following. At last I found the house which, from the description, must be the one belonging to Ephraim. I heard voices inside, trusted in the Madonna's protection, and knocked. A while passed before anyone came. I knocked again. Light seeped through the shutters.

'"Who's knocking?" asked a voice, light and youthful.

'"A poor monk of the Pauline order," I replied.

'"What do you want?"

'"I seek shelter for myself and my dog; I am tired and hungry and freezing …"

'The door opened a crack. A girl of about fourteen looked at me with brown, old–wise eyes.

'"We've a house full of foreign soldiers,' she whispered. 'Are you what you claim to be?"

'"Yes," I said. "My name is Jan, Brother Jan."

'"And you're not a deserter?" she asked. "All sorts come around these days."

'"No."

'She studied me again. "Can you pay? We only take roubles; lodging is three roubles."

'"That's expensive," I said, disheartened. I had only two German marks left of my travel money.

'She slammed the door in my face.

'"For Christ's mercy," I pleaded.

'"We are Jews," came a voice from behind the door, and I heard her laugh.

'Then I remembered the pouch of jewels I carried on my chest. They belonged to the Madonna, but I had to use them to help us on our flight to safety. I knocked again.

'"I have no money," I said, "but I have valuables; a diamond or a pearl I can give in place of money."

'So eager was I to get into that cursed house. She didn't answer at first. Then I heard shuffling steps inside and a rusty voice said, 'Let me see your diamonds.'

'The door opened slightly. I opened the pouch, groped around, and found the smallest one. Ephraim turned and twisted it in the light of a flickering lantern hanging in the hallway.

'"I'll give you a night's lodging for this stone," he said. "It's not worth much, but I'll do it anyway."

'"Three roubles?" I objected. "You can't mean to give me only three roubles for it; it's worth a hundred." I didn't actually know its value; I just said a number.

'"Your dog is included," he said tiredly, shaking his grey dangling curls. His kaftan was old and shiny with grease, and the diamond glittered between his yellow fingers.

'I stood by the door, uncertain, but I couldn't go any further. I had to be indoors. My legs were aching, my back was in pain; I would soon collapse.

'"Besides, you'll get three roubles in cash and a meal for you and your dog," he added when he saw me hesitate.

'He had swindled me shamelessly, but I couldn't take any more. I had reached my limit, and there were many of the Madonna's jewels, a whole pouch full. I nodded and stepped inside. I carried the well–wrapped icon with me. I was shown to a room high up under the roof; it was cold and gloomy, but far better than being outside. I placed the icon behind my bed and lay down on it for a moment. I fell asleep immediately.

'I had perhaps slept a couple of hours when I awoke to someone watching me. I sprang up; the Jewish girl was standing in the middle of the room.

'"I came here once before," she said, "but you were fast asleep. If you want food, come down to the taproom; we've cooked a pot of meat, there's enough for everyone."

'I got up, washed my hands, and went downstairs. In the taproom sat the nine soldiers; the nine riders Soten just spoke about. One of them had his shoulder bandaged. They were in the middle of a meal. I greeted them, took a seat, and said my monastery's table prayer. No one took notice of me; no one spoke to me, and they didn't speak much to one another either. I understood they were tired and had travelled far. After the meal, most went to their rooms; I heard a couple snoring and the wounded man groaning.

'Two remained seated by the stove. Those who remained in the taproom were the same who sit here now: Kunicke, Krebs, and I, Brother Jan of the Pauline order. The two soldiers made themselves quite at home in the room and took it over. They fetched warm water, trimmed their beards and shaved, and splashed soap all over the floor. And one of them, Kunicke – no, let me just call him by his proper name – Winterstein, disappeared and returned with a bottle of wine and some tin mugs.

'"Will you drink a glass of wine with us?" he asked me politely. "It'll do you good if there's still cold in you."

'I thanked him; I was unsure whether to accept, but he had already poured. We toasted; I'd never drunk wine before. It was sweet and strong; a mild, pleasant warmth spread through me and did me good. I suddenly felt safe; something told me I was among civilised people and that at least for the time being, I was safe. The devil whispered in my ear.

'"The landlord offered me a diamond for two hundred roubles," Winterstein said to his comrade.

'"And what did you answer?" said the other.

'"I asked if he'd gone mad. True, today for the first time we're human beings again; we've shaved, washed, and got rid of most of the lice. We've a glass of wine on the table and are living in something close to luxury, but there's still a long way from that to diamonds …"

'"That might have been my diamond," I interjected. "I had no money and had to give it to him for three roubles and board and lodging."

'"You speak German?" said Winterstein's comrade.

'"That swine," shouted Winterstein and began to curse Ephraim; I had never heard such swearing before, and I blushed.

'"Forgive me," he suddenly said, "I forgot you were here. A soldier's language is sometimes rather expressive. But I'll help you!"

'And he began yelling and calling for the landlord, who appeared at once; he had probably been listening. Winterstein sternly asked why he only wanted to give me three roubles and board for a stone he himself wanted two hundred for. He called him a swine and a usurer who exploited the misfortune of travellers.

'He didn't let Ephraim get a word in; he was indignant on my behalf. "Bring the stone!" he suddenly shouted. Ephraim protested, but in the end, the stone was brought forth. Eventually, he agreed to pay me a further twenty roubles for it. It was kind of these strangers to take up my cause. Perhaps I could join them and travel under their protection.

'When the bottle was empty, I tested the waters.

'"I don't know much about this," I said, "but if the wine can be had here, maybe I could order another bottle. You mustn't take it the wrong way; I just mean that since I've now received so much money …"

"'Thank you, young friend,' said Winterstein. "We accept gladly; but you must keep us company for a while."

'Then I remembered the image standing in my chamber above, and I had no peace until I had brought it down so I knew it was safe.

"'Ah, there's your luggage,' the two of them said cheerfully as I returned with it; it was still well–wrapped.

"'Yes, one can never be too sure,' I said.

"'So, you belong to the Pauline order?' said Winterstein a little later. He was sitting and playing with a pencil, drawing on the unpainted table.

"'Here is your order's coat of arms,' he suddenly said. "A raven and two lions, isn't that right?"

"'Yes,' I said, surprised. "How do you know of it?"

'He chuckled. "Saint Paul lived ninety years as a hermit in the desert," he said, "and a raven brought him his food. When he died, he was buried by two lions."

"'You know our Church?' I asked, astonished.

'He poured more wine into the mugs. It began to go to my head.

"'I know at least that your order has in its custody one of the world's most beautiful and rarest Madonna icons,' he said. "I mean the Black Madonna, supposedly painted by the Evangelist Luke immediately after Mary's death. It was painted on cedarwood and hangs in the monastery church at Jasna Gora."

"'No,' I said, "it is painted on cypress wood—"

'Winterstein insisted on his version and explained that he had studied art history before the war broke out. He had specialised in our Church's old devotional paintings of Byzantine origin. He denied that Luke had painted that image and instead mentioned other painters from whom it might have come, but he hadn't seen the icon himself – only reproductions – and had read a dissertation on it. Had I only let him keep his belief – the matter was trivial – but he spoke warmly and enthusiastically about paintings I had seen and mentioned icons that belonged to our order. The wine made me forget my caution, it made me bold and stirred a desire to boast about my mission and knowledge. I had some familiarity with these things myself.

'"The painting is on cypress wood,' I said. 'My monastery owns a painting done on the same type of wood, namely the famous Blue Madonna."

'"I think you're mistaken," he said again. "Besides, I've heard of that painting; it is supposed to be a wonderful work of art."

'"I have seen it every day for three years," I boasted. "I can see it before my eyes when I close them."

'And instinctively I placed my hand on the wrapped panel beside me.

'"Describe it to me," he said.

'Then the devil leaned over my shoulder, the wine burned through me, and no righteousness stood by my side. In my folly, I leaned forward over the table and knocked over a goblet with my arm, so the red wine dripped onto the floor.

'"You shall see her," I said. "You've been kind to me; you shall see her tonight."

'He didn't take me seriously at first – perhaps I was already a little drunk – he asked instead that his comrade refill the goblet I had knocked over.

'You shall see her immediately,' I insisted and began to unwrap.

Brother Jan fell silent. There was absolute quiet among us as we sat on Hasselbakken's veranda. The rain had stopped, the clouds had split here and there, and pale stars shone through the clear sky, already showing a faint light of the coming day. Jan's face was grey, the sharp features like they had been carved in wood. Only his eyes were alive; a dangerous glow smouldered in them. But his voice was composed as he turned to Winterstein:

'You said earlier that you must reserve the right to speak,' he said. 'Please, it is now your turn. Tell us truthfully what happened in Olesko that evening.'

CHAPTER VII

All eyes turned to Winterstein. He sat motionless in the armchair, his fingertips pressed together as a cool, ironic smile played around his mouth. He nodded faintly to Adrian and shrugged.

'Very well,' he said. 'I will continue; but it will not be the continuation of the young, inexperienced, and innocent story our monk just told us. I will follow up where Soten ended. For there was more than war then; there was defeat, revolution and dissolution, not only outwardly, but within us all. Fine, let's recall events, but let's be fair! If the dead are to be summoned, then we, the living, must be too, as we were then.'

He looked around. His words had impact; the man was right.

'For years we had fought out in the East, in mud, filth, and misery, and slowly we had been broken down. Everything bright within us had withered; no rays of light shone upon us from outside. But we held on, because it was our duty and because we were fighting for our country.

'Then suddenly everything collapsed. We found ourselves abandoned deep within enemy territory. The population, who had played both sides and at times even greeted us as liberators, suddenly rose against us and became enemies. They ambushed us and murdered our wounded; from all sides came reports of atrocities, and the future was hidden behind clouds thicker and darker than the ones we have seen here tonight.

'No laws applied anymore, no bonds held; only evil thrived, only the strong and amoral could assert themselves in this terrible world of defeat. Yes, I remember that evening in Olesko. I remember every second and every mood. I remember the luxury of being able to shave, wash, and stretch out in a warm room filled us with a wonderful sense of wellbeing. We were like intoxicated men, drunk on gentle, fine wine – we felt like we had returned to life – that's how I felt, and I believe Adrian felt the same.'

Adrian nodded; a candle flickered and went out.

'Since we left Daudsewas, we dragged ourselves forward like animals. We had not spoken much; we looked at each other with suspicion. We were strangers, from different nations. We knew that some of our soldiers had joined the Reds and some the Whites; we didn't know our neighbour's mindset and could not trust him.

'I had a vague sense that Adrian and I had some shared past. He was a musician, I had studied art history; the same hunger grew in us both, hunger for … for … Well, simply put, hunger for beauty! And the little bit of comfort that grew in us that evening in the wretched inn finally washed over us like a surging flood.'

He paused for a moment.

'I have often thought about that evening,' he continued, 'and I've tried to understand why certain dreadful things happened. I can't explain it any other way …'

His voice sounded thoughtful and sorrowful; he spoke slowly and deliberately. Then he broke off and continued briskly and harshly:

'In short, we felt good – damn good in fact – and when a young monk appeared, we pulled him into our conversation. Perhaps he's just an ordinary, ignorant beggar monk, I thought when I saw him, but perhaps he's a man with knowledge. Sometimes you meet such people among Russian monks, and that was what I was longing for.

'We began to talk about painting, images, and icons; he was well – versed in his subject. The conversation excited me, my blood ran quicker; the rather good Crimean wine the host had probably helped. And then the miracle happened; the monk bent down and began to unwrap the paper covering a large package he carried with him. A marvellous cabinet came into view – we have all seen it – but back then, in those surroundings, it filled our wretched existence with heavenly light … Then he opened the panel, and the Madonna of Heaven turned her eyes upon us … My heart stopped. I couldn't breathe. Everything gripped me: the glorious colours in jubilant blue, the vibrant, shining eyes, the quiet, hidden, happy half–smile.'

'Yes, you can understand a bit of it,' Winterstein said suddenly, turning to me. 'Nefertiti.'

I simply nodded. Winterstein continued.

'Adrian and I stood up. In the first few minutes neither of us spoke; the same feeling filled us both. The monk had fallen to his knees before the image. Then the door opened and the host crept in with staring, fixed eyes; and I was suddenly jolted back into reality. Only in that moment did it strike me that it posed a danger to us; that the priceless Blue Madonna was in the same house as us. Only then did I realise that the painting was worth a fortune.

'Something stirred in me; a wild thought began to grow. I tried to push it away but it came back; it filled my head completely and paralysed me with its horror. Meanwhile Adrian took charge and got the host out of the room. 'Where are you coming from, and where are you going?' I asked the monk; I could not recognise my own voice.

'He told us and hinted that perhaps we could travel the same way. Meanwhile, thoughts chased each other in my head; it was a long journey to Jasna Gora, anything could happen to him on the way. Ignorant robbers could plunder him and toss the painting into the fire; it was inconceivable that he had even made it as far as Olesko. And from here into Austria, to peace, oblivion, and the future; it was only six or seven days' ride, if we took the shortest route …

'"I thank you," I told the monk; my voice was still hoarse and unnatural, and I avoided his gaze. "It has been a great experience;

may my comrades also be permitted to view your monastery's Madonna? They are just ordinary unrefined soldiers …"

'"Even the lowliest finds comfort with our Madonna," said the monk, and laughed joyfully on behalf of his Madonna and the impression she had made on us unbelievers. I woke my comrades; I spoke quietly, so no outsiders could hear me.

'"Something extraordinary has happened to us," I said. "The monk who dined with us is carrying a famous, remarkable painting. It's worth a fortune; I know something about such things—"

'"How much?" someone asked.

'"I can't say exactly, but there are probably museums that would be willing to pay half a million—"

'Greed shone in their eyes; the thoughts of our difficult future, without money and education, had weighed on us like a crushing burden. I looked anxiously at Soten; he was, in a way, our leader, or at least the most practical, battle–seasoned man among us. Everyone looked at him and waited to hear what he would say. He stretched out so his bed creaked, then answered that he was damn reluctant; it smelled too much like a highway robbery.

'"Who are we taking this painting from?" I asked rhetorically. "Is it a private individual? Is it perhaps the monk who owns it? No, it's a monastery that has had millions in income from the painting over the years. It's owned by cowardly, treacherous, profiteering monks; a religious order with vast estates …"

'"I believe that fate has sent us this painting, that it would be madness not to make use of it." That's how I spoke, and I provoked the other men; they agreed with me, and Soten mostly gave in as well. "We've taken a machine gun and half a dozen horses," he said indifferently, "why not take a Madonna too? Very well, but I've done my share in acquiring the guns and horses. I'm a soldier, not a highway robber. I only ask that nothing be done to the little monk." And he pointedly turned over in his bed and put an end to the conversation.

'The rest of us agreed to leave immediately under cover of darkness. To succeed, we would have to ride through a dangerous area to get straight into Austria. Two men went out to fetch the horses and prepare for departure, while the rest of us entered the taproom to prepare for the difficult act that now lay ahead. Soten remained in bed.

'"It's not urgent," he said, "a soldier's first duty is to eat and sleep when he has the chance."

'The monk had placed the painting on a table in the corner and lit a candle on either side. It stood there, surrounded by a halo of heavenly blue light. I felt that the painting already had a tremendous power over me, that it was the key to all my happiness. I could no longer live a day without it. I stopped thinking of its value. Only a young, inexperienced monk stood between me and my painting; mine, I already thought, mine!

'"My young friend," I said to the monk, "have you thought about your responsibility in carrying this painting? Have you considered what might happen along the way?"

'"My life is in God's hands," he said simply.

'Boehm and Schneckenburger carried the machine gun out through the room, the others packed, and a couple stood silently before the painting. Even these rough soldiers forgot their misery and concerns in the presence of the power and noble peace radiating from this marvellous work of art.

'I continued clenching my teeth; I had to get through this. 'The first and best gang will take your Madonna from you; Red Guards will take pride in making a bonfire of it just because it belongs to the church, and ignorant soldiers will use it to stoke the fire. Have you thought about that?'

"'Yes,' he said quietly, "but I will give my life for it. I can do no more."

'Now I had to be cruel, I had to say it! I stepped right up to him and snapped: "Therefore we will relieve you of the burden and help you with the responsibility; do you understand?"

'Suddenly he realised what I meant and understood our preparations. He turned deathly pale and looked around helplessly, but met only hard faces and closed expressions.

"'Oh, Madonna, help me," he said tearfully.

'At my signal Krauter quickly stepped over and closed the panel. The monk tried to follow him, but I held him back. Suddenly he tore himself loose and screamed at the top of his lungs: "Help! Help! They are stealing the holy image; all good people, help me!"

'He rushed towards the door. Mayer tried to stop him, but the monk pushed him to the floor, and a chair overturned; all the while he screamed so loudly he could have woken the dead.

"'Stop!" I shouted and drew my pistol. "Stop!" But he didn't hear; he was senseless with agitation, terror, and despair.

He threw open the door and cried into the dark night: 'Help, help, to arms!'

'I fired. He clung to the door and screamed; I fired again. The monk stood for a moment, then fell heavily across the threshold. Mayer, who had gotten back on his feet, bent over him and shot him in the head to make him stop shouting. We rushed toward the exit; we had to step over the monk to get out.

"'Look here," Mayer suddenly said, "look what he's got on him ..." and he pulled out a pouch from the dead man's chest. It jingled; we forgot everything else and gathered around for a moment. It was jewels, pearls, diamonds, rubies ... they sparkled in a gleaming stream before our eyes.

'The monk lay at our feet, face down. Suddenly he stirred and said something. I bent down towards him, thinking he was dying.

'"Our Madonna has another name too," he said slowly and unclearly, "she is also called the Madonna of Vengeance."

———

'There was activity in the dark street; windows were thrown open, we heard voices and footsteps but saw no one. Our horses were ready.

'"Away!" someone shouted. We worked frantically in the darkness, fastened the machine gun and placed the panel on the opposite side of the pack.

'"Let's be done with it," we yelled in unison, as we cursed and stumbled and raged in wild panic.

'From somewhere in the darkness, two shots rang out. We were being fired upon; a bullet slammed into the wall behind us like a whip crack, a pane of glass shattered. Soten came calmly out the door as the last man. I heard his even voice.

'"Everyone here?" Then he called us by name, and we answered "yes" and "present". "Mount up!"

'There was the jingle of harnesses; new shots came from the right, as people were coming down the street. Suddenly I heard the familiar sound of a bullet striking. Before me a dark figure wavered in the saddle and fell to the ground; it was Mendel … We could not stop; we rode off as fast as we could.

'Soten released the safety on a couple of hand grenades and dropped them behind him. They exploded behind us with deafening crashes; clumps of earth flew into the air, windowpanes shattered, and our horses galloped off in terror. That was the beginning of the ride from Olesko.'

Winterstein fell silent and stared for a long time, blankly, at the golden horizon where the coming day emerged. The cloud cover slowly receded northward; the storm was over. In a moment the sun would rise in all its glory and majesty; it was eerie and unreal.

'All these years I thought the monk was dead,' said Winterstein suddenly, echoing what he had just recounted.

Jan lifted his head; his face was ravaged, grey, and sorrowful. In the light of the first faint sunray, I saw a thin, bitter smile on his face. 'You are right,' he said, 'the little monk truly died. A young, faithful, trusting monk lost his life that night in Olesko.'

———

Anne Marie filled my thoughts for a long time as I saw her that morning when we finally set off. It had been a long and emotionally exhausting night. The clear grey morning light pushed everything into the distance. Anne Marie stood on the veranda steps in her simple, white dress; her face was tired and serious, but her hair flamed red in the morning sun. Soten, Jan and I walked together; the two were to spend the night at the hotel. I helped them wake the hotel staff and arrange a room. Then I went straight home.

My landlady was already up. She came to meet me in the hallway. 'There seems to be something going on at Hasselbakken,' she said, 'I was asked to tell you to phone immediately.' I rang and heard Adrian's voice:

'You have to come over again,' he said, 'something has happened. We went upstairs to go to bed right after you left, and Winterstein went to his room. Suddenly we heard a heavy fall. I hurried to his room and found him lying on the floor. I think he is dead; he's not breathing. I have sent for a doctor.'

'When did it happen?' I asked.

'I think it must have been about ten minutes after you left.'

CHAPTER VIII

I arrived at Hasselbakken together with the doctor; he caught up with me and asked if he could offer me a lift. Adrian was completely confused; he spoke nonstop as we walked upstairs. He explained that he had left Winterstein lying the way he had found him; he had only turned him over. Winterstein was lying face down on the floor, and Adrian had been afraid that he might not be able to breathe if he was still alive. The doctor said he could have laid him on a sofa.

'He was too heavy for me,' said Adrian.

Winterstein lay on the floor, looking as if he were sleeping; he still had his cool, ironic smile. The doctor knelt and examined him, then asked me to help, and together we lifted the dead man onto a sofa. While the doctor continued his examination, I looked around the room. There were no signs of disturbance. The door to the veranda was apparently open, but we all slept with the windows open in this season; there was nothing unusual about that.

The Blue Madonna stood on a table in the corner. I went over and looked at her; the panel was open. The night's stories had filled my imagination to the brim; it seemed to me that she had a different expression than the last time I saw her. She now looked more serious, more melancholy, and the expression in her eyes had become dark and deep as an abyss; but the night had been long, and its events had naturally affected me. Before my eyes I saw the dark taproom in Olesko, the two poor, flickering candles, and the monk's terrible story still echoed in my ears.

That's how it is with great works of art, I thought; we sense our own innermost and unconscious world in them, far more than we can comprehend in a cool, sober morning hour. They strike sparks from us and feed our innermost flame, and so we blaze, each according to our humble means, God help us.

'Excellent painting,' said the doctor, who had risen from the sofa. 'Is it yours?' he asked Adrian.

Adrian explained that it belonged to Winterstein; he asked if he was dead.

'Yes, that is certain,' said the doctor.

'Were you together last night?'

We explained that we had just left each other when the incident happened.

'Did you notice anything unusual about him?'

We had to deny it.

'Was he agitated? Did the conversation touch on anything that might have given him, for instance, a shock or affected him psychologically? I ask in case he had a weak heart.'

Adrian left it to me to answer.

'Yes,' I said, 'I do believe the conversation was quite upsetting for Winterstein. We spoke about the old days during the war, and rather dreadful things were brought up.'

Adrian nodded in confirmation. The doctor examined the dead man again.

'It may, of course, be due to other internal causes,' he said. 'But the most likely is cardiac paralysis; I think my report will state that.' He then asked some more general questions.

The doctor was about to leave when Soten and Jan arrived; Adrian had notified them by phone. He introduced them to the doctor as old war comrades who were here on holiday. They were pale and silent. It clearly affected them to see the man they had spent a long, intense night with on Hasselbakken's veranda, lying there lifeless and motionless.

'He was once our comrade,' mumbled Soten.

Jan said nothing, but I observed that he made the sign of the cross. Then he noticed the Madonna's image and bowed in reverent greeting. He remained standing in deep contemplation in front of it while we spoke of the more mundane and practical matters about the death.

Soten hinted at some knowledge of Winterstein's family situation; it was a blessing for us. I write 'us' because I assumed that the lion's share of arrangements would fall on me; Adrian usually left such affairs to Anne Marie or me.

'We must of course send a telegram to someone,' I said.

'Winterstein's wife died five years ago,' said Soten, 'and after that his three children died, one each year. He had this Madonna in his care, but he had to pay for it with his earthly happiness. I know he has an old sister somewhere; the safest and simplest is to notify the embassy.'

It was a strange remark, but I didn't dwell much on it in my exhausted state. I asked after Anne Marie, but she had gone to bed; I suggested that we follow her example, and then meet again later that day at my place. Jan was still standing in front of the image. He flinched, as if returning from another world, when Soten spoke to him. He straightened up, again made the sign of the cross, and closed the panel slowly, carefully and reluctantly, as though he was unwilling to leave the image.

My sleep was deep, heavy, and without dreams.

———

We were quiet and a little strained when we met again; it was perhaps only natural that we found it difficult to strike the right tone. Last evening had turned into a reckoning between the dead man and the two strangers. The situation was eased somewhat by the fact that they didn't act as though they were particularly affected by the death. I had informed the embassy .

'But what are we supposed to do now?' asked Adrian; he was entirely helpless in such matters.

'For now, we'll wait and see,' I said, 'we'll surely hear from the right party.'

'It was strange, his death,' said Anne Marie quietly to herself, 'especially after what we heard about him last night.'

'It was fate,' said Jan briefly.

'What do you mean?' I asked.

Suddenly Soten's remark about how Winterstein had to pay with his earthly happiness flashed before me.

'An evil deed carries its own seed,' said Jan gravely, 'and sooner or later Nemesis appears. Winterstein had his time; it just took a long time for fate to catch up with him.'

'But didn't his wife and children die?'

'Yes,' said Soten. 'For a time Winterstein had everything a person could wish for in terms of earthly happiness. He was a successful businessman, and he had a very good reputation as an art historian. Then suddenly everything went wrong for him. First his wife died,, and at the same time he lost his great fortune. Finally, he became involved in a case that damaged him greatly. He had guaranteed a van Dyck that was purchased by the Louvre for a very large sum. But the painting turned out to be a forgery. He took it very hard. He no longer had a lucky hand.'

'But he was still fairly well off?' asked Jan, 'that was the impression I got from what he said.'

'Yes,' said Soten, 'he still had some money left, but it wasn't much.'

'You and Mr. Soten had no reason to hold him in high regard,' said Anne Marie again, turning to Jan.

'*De mortuis nil nisi bene*', he mumbled simply. 'Let us not speak ill of the dead.'

'But Winterstein mentioned something last night about a "Madonna of Vengeance," continued Anne Marie.

Jan stared straight ahead. 'We believe in our order that the church punishes itself,' he said evasively. 'He was not a good man. He was no better to his own than he was to me.'

It was as if Anne Marie had suddenly remembered something. 'We stopped in Olesko,' she said, 'but we never found out what became of you after that—'

Jan looked at her with a peculiar expression; it was not unfriendly, but it was hard to define. 'Let's empty the cup,' he said, 'it seems like fate.' He looked at Soten, who returned his gaze.

'It's not for me to tell anymore,' said Soten with the same wolfish smile I had noticed on him before. 'I didn't accompany them that far.'

'Winterstein said it would take six or seven days to reach the border,' said Anne Marie.

'And there were nine riders,' said Jan.

'Yes, but Mendel was shot outside the inn,' said Soten. 'After that, there were only eight.

'I was only with them the first three days. I had a legitimate reason to leave, so I don't know exactly who reached the border or when the survivors crossed over—'

There was a meaningful pause. I found myself looking at Adrian; soon, everyone looked at him. He was very pale, with large beads of sweat on his forehead.

'So it's clearly your turn,' said Anne Marie. 'If only you had told us earlier …'

What she meant by that last part I didn't quite understand; or rather, I began to wonder about the implications. Then Soten said that he could continue the account up to when he left the party , and perhaps Adrian would then take over.

Adrian looked like a condemned man who had been granted a one–hour reprieve; he kept wiping his face with his handkerchief. Anne Marie glanced over at him from time to time.

'We covered many miles that first night,' began Soten in his terse tone. 'The weather was hellish; it snowed and gales blew; the wet snowflakes melted against our clothes. We finally reached some tolerable trenches that the peasants had used to store potatoes; we spent another day there. When night fell, we rode on. The terrain was hilly, with ridges and valleys. We had little visibility.

'Around midday the following day, we realised we were being followed. We saw a small cavalry patrol tracking us on either side of the ridge. They were Cossacks; we could tell by their long lances. We had to shake them somehow. An idea came to me as we rode up through the valley and approached the ruins of an old mill, a farmstead, or whatever it was. Roughly 300 metres in front of it lay a deep ravine, ideally suited as cover for anyone wanting to assault the mill. I was used to reading the landscape that way, which is why I noticed it. On the left–hand side, there was a long stretch of forest with quite a bit of undergrowth.

'If we placed the machine gun in the forest and concealed it, while simultaneously staging a mock skirmish from the ruins, we'd have a good chance of drawing the enemy into the ravine, where they could be bombarded. I made my arrangements; my comrades followed my lead, and even Schneckenburger was cooperative. I placed him, Boehm, and Mayer in the ruins. Winterstein and … and Krebs got the machine gun. I took up position to cover it along with Schulz and Krauter.

'The Cossacks advanced cautiously. Shots were fired at them from the ruins; they dismounted, and shortly after their main force arrived, a sotnia of 100 men, or something similar. They advanced carefully, as I had expected. Schneckenburger, Boehm, and Mayer fired eagerly and made hits now and then. The Cossacks moved up in short bursts, and some of them had already gathered in the ravine. On both flanks, patrols advanced on foot; we would soon be under attack.

'I waited as long as I could, then gave the signal to Winterstein to begin firing. We ourselves opened fire on the nearest patrol. But the machine gun was silent; the weapon that was supposed to save us failed to speak! Now *we* were in the trap! We jumped up and ran for our lives back to the machine gun; bullets whizzed past us. The two were in the process of loading the machine gun onto the horse! I asked Winterstein what the devil he was doing. He said they had a jam, and that the only thing to do was to get away. "But what about our comrades?" I shouted. He shrugged. He had his pistol ready, otherwise I would have struck him down.

'At that moment, the Cossacks charged the ruins with loud hurrahs; their patrol had nearly encircled the position from the far side. It was hopeless; we could do nothing. We couldn't come to the aid of our three comrades and had to leave them to certain death. But those three must have believed in their dying moments that I had abandoned them. What else could they think? And so Schneckenburger, Boehm, and Mayer died. Five of us were left. Suspicion smouldered and gnawed at me; I examined the machine gun the first time we rested. I could find no reason for the jamming; it appeared to be in full working order. Winterstein watched my inspection darkly. But there were only five of us; we had to stick together.

'The next afternoon we suddenly encountered a Cossack patrol in woodland. We hadn't managed to lose them . We returned fire, and they fled. But Krauter had taken a bullet through his thigh and was bleeding heavily. We dressed the wound and tied him to his horse. We had to move on; death was at our heels. We rode for hours in pitch darkness, now and then striking matches to orient ourselves by the compass. It was bitterly cold but clear. Our eyebrows and beards were frosted; we could see our breath like white smoke. Krauter was afraid of frostbite in the wound and moaned occasionally. At times, he lost consciousness.

'At last, we reached some houses that, according to the map, must have been on the outskirts of Stowovjeny. We chose one that was off the beaten track and hoped to rest there until daylight; our horses were very worn out and often stumbled from fatigue. We had to get indoors. An old woman opened the door after we had knocked for some time. She understood a little German. It turned out we were in the right village and on the right road. She was reluctant to take us in, but we didn't negotiate long; we went straight in and made ourselves at home. Then we saw to the horses, posted a guard, collapsed on the floor, and slept as only the dead can.

'At dawn, the guard woke us and reported that we were surrounded. He had heard hoofbeats and seen shadows in the morning mist. I was too sleepy for it to make much of an impression. Our only chance now was to fight our way out. If it became necessary, we would even have to sacrifice the machine gun. This formed the basis of my plan. The house had a trapdoor in the roof. From there, we could command the nearest surroundings and the plain behind the house. Schulz and I, who had the best horses, were to cover the retreat; Winterstein and Krebs were to take care of the wounded Krauter and the icon. We agreed on this; they were to ride to the nearest village to the west and wait for us there. I calculated that I could hold the position for a while using the machine gun, then cover our retreat with hand grenades. After that, fate would have to be on our side.

'Schulz and I climbed up to our trapdoor and observed the environs. We saw some indistinct figures through the haze and heard voices; everything was ready. I gave the signal. We heard hoofbeats; our comrades rode off … There were a couple of shots through the mist, then a few distant shouted commands; several riders came galloping around the corner and sped out across the plain in pursuit of our comrades. I bent over the machine gun, aimed ahead of the horses and gave them a long burst. It was over in an instant; they were swept away and tumbled over one another. We had to seize the moment; we threw a couple of hand grenades down the alleys to the right and left and rushed down to our horses. Our task was accomplished; we had covered the retreat!

'In the garden behind the house lay the wounded Krauter, unconscious on the ground. Winterstein and Krebs were gone, but they had taken our horses with them! I ran around the corner to see if the horses might have broken loose. Shots rang in from all sides now – I had to take cover and ran back inside. Schultz lay in the middle of the floor. He had been shot through the head. I was alone; I heard the Cossacks storming in … At that moment, I discovered a hatch in the floor. Almost instinctively, I opened it and jumped down. I found myself in a cellar; I crawled as far in as I could and found shelter behind a large stone. There I lay for two days, not daring to come out …'

A deep, painful silence followed when he finished. Adrian had the floor; we were waiting for it, and he felt it. But he couldn't form a coherent story. He shook his head and began by saying that he had hoped never to be forced to speak of those horrors, and then he fell silent again. We sat waiting; the quiet was unbearable. He spoke again.

'Yes, it's true that Winterstein and I were behind the machine gun, but he was the one who was meant to fire. Suddenly, he said it had jammed and that we couldn't stay there any longer. I could see in his eyes that he was lying, but what could I do? And that morning in Nowovjeny I didn't know we were going to leave Krauter behind, I swear I didn't know. I was already in the saddle when Winterstein lifted Krauter down and laid him on the ground. "He's done for," he said. I didn't look at him. Then he took the other three horses and whispered to me through clenched teeth: "It's about the painting, for God's sake!" Everything happened as if through a fog; I was untethered from reality, and I believed Winterstein when he said the three who stayed behind had no chance of escape …'

Again, that oppressive silence. Suddenly Adrian shouted: 'I'm an artist; I never asked to be part of this. I loathe it; I felt degraded, I felt like an animal. I am not obliged to shoot and kill …'

No one said anything.

'I was passive,' Adrian continued in a high, hysterical voice, 'who today can blame me for doing nothing; for not lifting a finger to commit murder!'

Adrian's eyes were completely wild.

Anne Marie suddenly said, as though she were looking past him, 'And since then, Mr. Soten, what then?'

'After two days, I dared to come out,' said Soten gruffly. 'I was hungry and freezing, and I looked the part; the old woman thought I was a ghost. With a suitable mix of persuasion and threats, I prevented her from reporting me. I found out that the Cossacks had looted Krauter and Schulz and taken the machine gun, and then immediately set off in pursuit of the other two; no one had considered that someone might be hiding. That same night I moved on, alone. A few days later, I fell into the hands of the Ukrainian General Petlyura's troops and was given the choice: die or join them. I was given the rank of second lieutenant; that was the beginning.'

'And you,' said Anne Marie thoughtfully, turning to me, 'what do you make of all this?'

'It both frightens and impresses me,' I said after a moment. 'There are greater forces in man than are dreamt of in your philosophy, Horatio,' I added, with a failed attempt at quoting *Hamlet.*

'There was no happiness in it,' Jan mumbled. 'From the first moment, fortune turned its back on the nine robbers; seven of them perished, and only two made it through.'

'And you?' asked Anne Marie. 'You were abandoned on the threshold of the inn in Olesko; how is it that you're still alive? You were shot in the head.'

Jan let his fingers glide lightly over the large scar on his chin.

'They didn't aim well enough,' he said matter-of-factly. 'Afterwards, the Jewish girl took care of me; she nursed me faithfully for two months, then I recovered. But one day the Red troops conquered the town. I was given the same choice as Soten, and had to join them as a volunteer; I had no choice, no future. I was a lost monk, a man who had failed his holiest duty.'

His face once again took on that marked, almost embittered expression. Adrian sat down in the living room and started fiddling with the radio. He searched for foreign stations, but got no usable reception. There was constant static and interference, as the weather had completely gone off the rails that summer; it had been too hot.

CHAPTER IX

Then the fog rolled in, and lingered for several days. During that time, I saw nothing of Adrian and Anne Marie, although I was eager to hear from them. Adrian called one day but he had nothing to say, and wanted nothing from me. He told me that the probate court had intervened at the embassy's request and made an inventory of Winterstein's belongings.

'Isn't that rather strange?' I asked.

'It was done at an explicit request,' Adrian replied. From whom, he did not say. But he told me Winterstein was to be buried the next day, a Wednesday.

I went to the funeral. It was a foggy day with a little rain. The little country graveyard lay wet and dreary beneath the poplars. Only a few were present; Winterstein had died in a foreign land, so naturally it could not be any other way. A wreath had arrived from his sister.

A taxi was waiting for the others. No one invited me to join; perhaps there wasn't room. There were five people in all; Arvid Falk was with them. Still, I felt a bit slighted. Anne Marie had greeted me briefly, but barely said a word. At a funeral, perhaps it isn't easy, but still … I remembered that Anne Marie had once spoken to me about herself and Adrian. She had said that he was kind and a good man, and that she was glad to have someone she could completely trust, and who, no matter what happened, was her friend.

'And what about me, then?' I had replied.

'That's true,' she said then, and took my hand and pressed it. But perhaps you can't really count on moments like that.

I stayed at home those days. Something might happen; someone might send for me, or the phone might suddenly ring. The fog wrapped everything in its clammy veil; it blocked all views and mercilessly locked me in with my own dark thoughts. I couldn't shake the impression of that long and harrowing night. It haunted me. I kept thinking about what had happened, about fate suddenly intervening and Nemesis catching up with Winterstein so many years later.

And strangely enough, though I had seen the icon only briefly, it was the face of the Blue Madonna that kept following me, as if she demanded something of me. I saw her eyes before me and kept reliving that intense pain in her features, that never–resting strife in her gaze. But perhaps it was just the fog; it crept in with the air and filled every breath. I'm sometimes sensitive to long spells of bad weather; sometimes I've taken to bed to wait for sunnier days. I have the time for that.

One morning I was suddenly visited by Arvid Falk. He apologised for bothering me; but wanted to ask a question.

'I can tell you in strict confidence,' he said, 'that Adrian Krebs has approached me. He believes his life is in danger. What do you think about that? I know you are a friend of his and his wife's, and that you also know the story of the painting. Do you think his life is really in danger, or are his nerves playing tricks on him?'

I thought for a moment. 'I can only think that it must be his nerves,' I said.

Falk remained seated; he clearly had something on his mind.

'I can't say that I'm satisfied with the situation at Hasselbakken,' he finally said. 'I know nothing; I can't point to anything specific, although there are, in fact, quite a few peculiar incidents in this affair. My instincts have given me a bad feeling before and as it turned out, rightly so!'

'What are you referring to in particular?' I asked cautiously.

'For example, this sudden friendship,' said Falk. 'When I first got involved in this case, it was perfectly clear that there was no friendship between Winterstein and the two who arrived …'

'I've thought the same,' I replied.

'It was perfectly obvious,' Falk continued, 'that Winterstein already anticipated that those two would try to steal the painting. At Adrian's request, I travelled out to Hasselbakken. The first thing Winterstein told me was that two foreigners would be arriving, either by train or plane in the next few days. I was to keep an eye on them, wherever they went and whatever they did. He even gave me a photograph of them—'

A thought struck me. 'Where was it taken?' I asked.

'It was at least developed in Cologne,' he replied. 'There was a stamp on the back.'

'Yes, forgive me for interrupting,' I said.

'Well then; Winterstein was clearly aware of the danger. And he insisted on installing the most modern alarm systems, regardless of the cost. At the same time, I discreetly got in contact with the police, so the two could be intercepted if they attempted to leave the country. He asked me repeatedly whether everything was in place and whether he could rely on our police to stop them. I told him he could count on it; my people had them well under surveillance.'

'So the police weren't directly involved?' I asked. 'You mean it was just your private agency?'

Falk nodded. 'Yes, he didn't want the police involved unless it became absolutely necessary. Up to that point, everything was straightforward. But then this sudden *friendship developed* …'

'After the break-in,' I prompted.

Falk searched in his inner pocket. 'Have you seen the pictures?' he asked.

I shook my head. He took out a series of small photographs and arranged them in order. They were numbered. They showed Winterstein's room and the corner where the icon stood. They were quite dark and blurred . Only in the sixth photo could I make out a figure halfway into the frame. But in the ones that followed, the figure became completely clear. It moved closer to the iconwhile the camera kept taking pictures; finally, it stood in front of the Madonna, three images in a row showing this. A faint line betrayed the beam of a torch. In the next photo, the figure had raised its arm towards the icon – the following two shots showed the same pose – then something had happened! The thief must have noticed something. In the next shot, he had turned his face straight towards the camera. I saw a pair of sharp, tense eyes looking directly at me, and then came a couple of completely blank shots; and after that, the room was empty in the rest. But it had been Jan's face I saw, no doubt about it.

'It's pretty conclusive,' said Falk. 'Jan, as you call him, came in to steal the icon. He's in the middle of opening it when he suddenly hears the camera's click, turns around and shines his torch towards the sound, but doesn't spot the lens; it was well–concealed. He's startled and disappears—'

'But the *friendship*,' I repeated. 'The next day, Winterstein invites those two to Hasselbakken. Had he perhaps already seen the photographs?'

Falk nodded. 'He saw them the next morning at eleven.'

'I was with them that evening,' I said. 'And there was nothing unusual in Winterstein's behaviour.'

Falk lit a cigarette and inhaled deeply from the first drag. He looked absent–mindedly around the room and repeated slowly: 'The friendship, you say; yes, that's exactly what troubles me. Not the friendship in itself and that it was struck the day after the break–in, since Winterstein is dead and he's no longer our concern; but the fact that the friendship continues …'

'Continues?' I said, puzzled.

Arvid Falk looked at me. 'Don't you know,' he said in his thin, dry voice, 'that Soten and Jan have moved into Hasselbakken?'

His words shocked and confused me; a leaden weight seemed to settle on my chest and made it hard to breathe. I pulled myself together and replied as apathetically as I could:

'No, I didn't know. But is there space up there now, considering Winterstein's room can't be used?'

I had the impression Falk was watching me closely from under half–closed eyelids.

'We're cramped,' he said. 'I'm staying there too; and we are all constantly watching each other!'

'Yes, yes,' I said, at a loss for anything else.

Falk dropped his cigarette. 'That's exactly the point,' he said. 'Krebs invites those two to live with him. And at the same time, he asks me to come over and keep an eye on his life!'

'How t is Anne Marie taking it?'

'She's cheerful and lively,' Falk replied indifferently. 'She keeps the mood up; to be honest, I think she sees this as a welcome bit of excitement. She probably isn't very deep, but you know her better than I do, of course?'

Falk lit a new cigarette; I got the impression he was studying me sharply while lighting up. I understood what he was after, and why he had come, but I didn't bother to help him.

'Perhaps,' I said. 'What do we know about women anyway, we old bachelors? You're not married either, if I've heard correctly?'

Falk smiled at me. 'Oh no, you may be right,' he admitted, and at once began talking about something else, but he soon circled back to the matter; he was was clearly eager to hear my opinion. But I didn't say much. I had become cautious; it wasn't my role to give this man information or tell him what I thought.

Still, Falk was an entertaining fellow, and we spent a few pleasant hours together. I asked him about his work and told him I had seen his name a few times in connection with difficult cases that had been solved. He seemed happy to hear this.

'I'm still relatively new in the job,' he said modestly. 'I could certainly have more experience. But I always work according to two principles: the psychological method and the technical one. Everything that research has so far discovered about the human psyche, I bring into play; and at the same time, I keep myself up to date with the latest technical tools.'

We discussed this for a while.

'Applied to our present case,' he added, 'it means that naturally there may be people who have a motive to harm our friend Adrian Krebs. But who can do such a thing in cold blood? That's the question. I believe that just as you can deduce from the traces of an act that something has taken place, you can also – based on the perpetrator's mental state, psychological possibilities, their past, environment, and so on – arrive at the same conclusions.'

'A new form of psychoanalysis?' I laughed.

'Why not?' he said seriously. 'By the way,' he added suddenly, 'have you noticed that a third party is on the scene in the Adrian Krebs affair?'

'No,' I said, truly surprised. 'What do you mean?'

But he backed off; he couldn't say anything definite. He had only wanted to hear my opinion. He expressed his gratitude, told me he had received valuable information, but now he had to leave. I sat for a while afterwards, thinking about what had been said. I couldn't see that Falk had got any information at all.

That evil fog was still there, but I had made up my mind: I would visit Hasselbakken later that same day. And since no one had invited me, I would come unannounced.

———

As I arrived at Hasselbakken, I immediately sensed the same odd atmosphere from the night of Winterstein's death,; the two adventurers still dominated and set the tone. Anne Marie was lively, but a little high–strung, whereas Adrian was quiet and said little, but he seemed pleased to see me, and welcomed me right away. I settled into the sofa. The chair I usually sat in was occupied by Soten.

Adrian asked me what I'd been up to in the past few days. I answered something vague.

'How's the machinery business going?' Anne Marie suddenly asked.

'Don't ask,' I replied. 'That windmill is what I live off; but I don't care how the sails turn, it's enough for me that they do.'

'Mr Wiig doesn't really have any mission in life,' Anne Marie said.

'No,' I agreed meekly. 'By God, I have no life mission, unless you count turning with the windmill as one.'

'A good image,' Anne Marie said again. 'A windmill and a weathervane; same thing, right, Adrian?'

Adrian grumbled and changed the subject. Something hard and indifferent had come over Anne Marie, a ruthless detachment she hadn't shown before. But I persisted and took up the thread again:

'Times may come when the windmill spins all of us around, Anne Marie,' I said.

'Yes, and then what?' she said. 'What do you have to rely on then, when everyone closest to you betrays you and spins along too?'

I didn't answer.

'Then you only have yourself to rely on,' she continued. 'And God help the weak in this world. I wish I were a man; it's a time for men, we women are superfluous. These past few days have changed everything for me. I see things with different eyes; I feel like I've been asleep until now.'

'It looks so peaceful on the surface here in your beautiful country,' said Jan with his melodic priest's voice.

Soten was half-dozing in my usual armchair.

'Mr Soten,' said Anne Marie suddenly, 'I would like you to tell Waldemar Wiig how the meeting at Heilige Lampe came about. It would undoubtedly interest him.'

I started. Adrian must have capitulated entirely; did Anne Marie know of my involvement in the affair? I had denied knowing anything when she questioned me. But on the other hand, I had been foolish enough to recount the brawl. Soten had straightened up in the chair as she addressed him. He was ready at once and began without hesitation.

He had returned to Germany for the first time since the war and had happened to think about the affair in Olesko. He had advertised in the newspapers and over the radio, and gone to Cologne, where Jan had sought him out well in advance of the meeting and revealed himself. At that time, Soten had not recognised Jan; that was all.

'So the meeting led to nothing?' asked Anne Marie.

She was restless in her questioning; she probed and enquired and wouldn't let it lie. It frayed her nerves. I looked at her uneasily.

'No,' answered Soten shortly, ' Winterstein had also taken precautions to avoid us finding out where he lived or his new name. Naturally, we understood that he had thrown his old name overboard.'

'Just like Adrian,' said Anne Marie harshly. She knew that too.

'As we left the restaurant, we were attacked by four men dressed in S.A. uniforms,' continued Soten, 'but as old soldiers, we managed reasonably well. It was, in fact, foolish of Winterstein to have used S.A. uniforms, as the authorities quickly understood the scheme and became very keen to catch the suspect behind the misuse of uniforms. We received considerable help from them.

'We may not have known the name Winterstein was hiding under, but we knew he was an art historian, perhaps even a collector. We also knew his approximate age. I went through a register of all German art historians and noted twenty or thirty who could fit. In the register, there was also a listing of their works and publications, and I found that a certain Dr Kunicke had, in 1923, written a dissertation on Russian church art and famous paintings and icons in Russian churches.

'I got hold of the dissertation and found the Blue Madonna described in detail. Then I tipped off the authorities, but Winterstein must have been warned, and he managed to obtain a passport to Norway in time. As I said, it was great foolishness on his part to get the police involved; otherwise, we would hardly have been able to get at him.

'He could have argued that it was a matter of a war trophy; he could also have claimed that the Pauline Order had been dissolved in Soviet Russia and that its properties and possessions had been confiscated. He could have delayed us with a long series of lawsuits; he had the means, we did not. He naturally must have known all this, but perhaps he thought he could scare us off.'

'But it was our right,' said Jan suddenly in a deep voice. 'The icon still belongs to the Holy Pauline Order to this very day!'

'And the jewels —' burst out Soten, '— the jewels?'

Jan turned towards him; their eyes met, and Soten said no more. Instead, Adrian continued:

'For God's sake,' he cried, 'when will this ever end? I can't take it anymore, these endless discussions that lead nowhere! I can't bear it, it's destroying me!'

CHAPTER IX

And he ran out of the room, slamming the door violently behind him. We all looked towards the closed door, Soten with a crooked smile, Jan with slightly raised eyebrows, Anne Marie's face closed and hard. Several awkward seconds passed in silence. Anne Marie had grown pale these past days; she looked unwell. It was hardly surprising. By all accounts, hell had broken loose at Hasselbakken. And I could do nothing; an invisible and insurmountable wall shut me out. I felt it every minute, and I regretted ever having gone there.

Jan moved to the piano and began to play. He preluded slowly and softly, and then the tones rose into a mighty hymn. I had never heard it before; it sounded foreign, strange, and unlike any church music I knew. Suddenly he turned around on the stool and asked if we had heard the hymn before. We all answered that we had not.

'It is the hymn of the Blue Madonna,' he said meaningfully, and his eyes shone with fanaticism. 'It was played every day between three and seven o'clock in the monastery at Borodjanka in honour of the image of the Mother of God. Fortunately, it has been preserved, and I have brought it with me; and this hymn shall never fall silent …'

He paused a little, and it was as if he were listening.

'Do you think she can hear it?' he asked, with a peculiar smile.

'You know,' I said, breaking off the uncanny direction the conversation was taking, 'lately I seem to have seen her eyes before me. Naturally, it's just my imagination; I've only seen the picture fleetingly.'

'Would you like to see it again?' he asked eagerly. 'Would you mind?'

'Thank you,' I said, 'if it's allowed.'

Jan still sat on the piano stool, facing us. He continued speaking; his eyes were shining, and his voice sounded distant and muted. It was as if he were still playing.

'Sometimes,' he said, ' it is as though I am still wandering through the monastery church in Borodjanka. The dim, gentle light falls slantwise through the blue stained–glass windows, the organ roars, and the monks sing the sombre hymn. Countless dragging footsteps are heard across the stone flags, and then the faithful kneel and hardly dare lift their worshipping eyes towards the Madonna of hope and light.

'It is the simple and good–hearted souls who kneel there; women and girls in headscarves, old men with tall hats and white beards, young men with large, wondering eyes. It is not the defiant, wild souls, not the proud and haughty ones, not those whom Satan later let loose when he sought to destroy the world. And the hymn swells heavily through the room, it is as if I am sleeping and only dreaming all that has happened since; the war, the disgrace. But still, through it all I see again the compassionate eyes of the Madonna and the gleam in her golden hair, and sometimes I think that I have seen a little of it in a human being, that there is something that reminds me …'

'I know it,' muttered Soten thoughtfully to himself; it was as if he was unaware the words had escaped him. ' I have experienced the same thing.'

It was more Jan's tone than his words that evoked the peculiar mood that now came over us. It smoothed out time, our worries disappeared, and I too sat there and suddenly knew it. And the face that I now saw before my eyes was no longer the Madonna's, but Anne Marie's. Was it the lulling, chanting tone in Jan's voice that did it, was it hypnosis or suggestion? I don't know; I only know that suddenly I felt an irresistible urge to see the icon once more. I felt that it was connected to all of us and that from now on I too was drawn into the circle, and that my future would be bound to the Madonna's fate. The feeling of something inevitable filled me.

'Let's see the icon,' I said suddenly; I did not recognise my own voice.

Soten stood up. 'Come,' he said simply, and reached out his hand towards Anne Marie. From the piano came a few resounding concluding chords; it was as though they accompanied what awaited. Jan joined us as we reached the stairs.

He showed us the icon. I couldn't help but think of Winterstein's rapture when I had first seen it. With him, it had been the mad delight of the art lover and connoisseur, mixed with the desperate triumph that the painting was his; though it was looted from temples and sanctuaries, it was Winterstein's! With Jan, it was different. With him, it was rapture, devotion, religious ecstasy; he belonged to the Madonna, not she to him. He showed us the panel's fine carvings, the inlaid mother–of–pearl fields, the delicate gold inlays barely visible to the naked eye. All was for her glory.

'Look here,' he said, showing us the Holy Trinity figures in pure gold. 'Place your hand here,' he asked me.

I followed his instruction, and gently laid my thumb and forefinger over the dove's head and turned it to the right. With a faint click, the panel opened, and the Madonna looked at us again with her beautiful, sorrowful face. We stood for a long time gazing at it. None of us said anything. I noticed that Anne Marie's eyes were filled with tears. Jan stood with bowed head; perhaps he was praying, his lips were moving. I glanced sideways; Soten was standing in the middle of the floor, his eyes fixed on Anne Marie …

A cough sounded behind us. Adrian stood in the doorway. 'Take a good look,' he said as if nothing had happened, 'we won't have the icon for much longer. A representative of the heirs, or creditors, or whatever it is, has just announced his arrival by telegram. He's coming the day after tomorrow from Berlin.'

'You received a telegram?' asked Anne Marie.

'Yes,' Adrian replied. 'That is, the embassy was telegraphed.'

'So another stranger,' I said sarcastically. I was close to asking whether Anne Marie had room for him as well, if he too was to lodge at Hasselbakken. 'No,' said Adrian, 'at least the name sounds Norwegian. The telegram, as far as I could tell on the phone, was signed by a certain Finn Bjelke—'

'Finn Bjelke,' I said. 'I feel like I've heard that name before.'

But I couldn't place it at that moment; I tend to forget things quickly.

CHAPTER X

The next day felt like waking up in a new and smiling world. Yesterday's cares faded with the fog. The sky was clear, blue and cloudless, and the air light and fresh. The storm had cleansed the air of all evil. Trees and bushes still hung heavy with raindrops that glittered in the sunlight.

I sat on my veranda reading. Later in the morning, I saw Anne Marie and her two cavaliers strolling down the road; Adrian wasn't with them. They had all the time in the world; they wandered lazily along. Once, Soten darted off the path and into a bush where he picked rosehips for Anne Marie and presented them with an exaggeratedly gallant bow. I could see it all clearly through my binoculars. I could also follow them when they turned off the road and took a footpath; I knew where it led. I had walked it myself, both alone and with Anne Marie.

So I put on my hat and went for a walk too. I followed the road through the valley where, from old times, barn owls nest, hence the name. Rightly so, for I've often heard owls hooting there at dusk. I continued past the sawmills along the river; there was sawdust everywhere, reminding me of a circus. I strolled on in a leisurely manner, surrounded by lush green fields. A lake glinted nearby, and life teemed all around: insects buzzed, birds sang, and a flock of crows took off reluctantly and sought refuge at the edge of a forest, where they sat like heavy black lumps swaying in the treetops.

The group came over the hilltop and down toward the road; grass and bushes almost hid them. They saw me and waved. It was a cheerful gathering; Soten and Jan were as giddy as two boys, and Anne Marie's cheeks were flushed with colour. I had heard them laughing loudly from a distance. Soten had learned a few

Norwegian words and phrases; he butchered the language horribly but got great laughs from it. For my part, I couldn't understand how it could be so funny again and again! I walked back with them because they urged me to, but I couldn't quite match their mood; I couldn't get into the spirit of things.

'You're so quiet,' Anne Marie said suddenly, with a tone of faint disdain.

'Excuse me—' I said.

'You're the kind of man who would apologise for existing at all,' she said in the same tone and turned to the others, continuing her chatter.

I walked beside them, feeling uncomfortable and unhappy, and in that mood, we parted ways. I walked home alone and thought that, really, I might as well move abroad for a while. I'd look into the possibility; at the very least, I could leave for a year.

When I got home, I called a friend. 'I've suddenly got the urge to go out tonight,' I told him. We agreed to meet at a restaurant for dinner. To hell with sitting out here in the country any longer!

———

I slept long and heavily the next morning; I had come home on the last train, as the evening had been lively. I heard my landlady try the door a couple of times while I was half–asleep. It was well into the day before I was finally dressed and ready. But I was determined to keep my resolution; I wouldn't live like a hermit anymore. I would go into town more often and enjoy myself. To begin with, I'd take the midday train; my friend and I had arranged to meet again after office hours.

Then the phone rang; it was Adrian. I could hear in his voice that something had happened.

'Could you come over right away?'

I was just about to leave; I'd miss nothing by going over, and my train wasn't due for another hour. So for Adrian's sake, I went. He met me halfway down the hill.

'I need to talk to you,' he said quickly and in a low voice. 'Something has happened again!'

He said it so strangely, I stared at him. 'Soten is lying dead up there,' he continued.

'Soten?' was all I managed.

'Yes, for God's sake, Soten! Soten is dead! Does that surprise you? Were you expecting someone else?' Adrian looked at me suspiciously.

'I wasn't expecting anything,' I said shortly. 'Tell me.'

We sat down on some stones. it struck me that we had sat in this very spot back when I had just returned from Cologne and Adrian had walked home with me at night. How much had happened since then!

'Go on,' I repeated.

Adrian chewed on a blade of grass; he clearly found it difficult to begin.

'How did it happen?' I asked, to get him started.

'No one knows,' he said. 'He was lying there this morning. Exactly like Winterstein!'

'You'll have to explain from the start,' I suggested.

From his account, it appeared that they had sat up together in the evening, had a few cups of tea, and then some mixed drinks; the two Germans preferred their whisky straight. They had agreed to turn in early and were in bed by eleven. Adrian and Anne Marie had slept heavily all night and only woke around ten the next morning. They got up, and when they heard nothing from Soten's room, Adrian went in to call him for breakfast. There he found Soten lying dead, fully clothed, on a sofa; Soten's room was next to the one Winterstein had had. He must have been dead for a long time; he was completely cold.

'And there was no sign ... of ...' I hesitated, '... that his death was not natural?'

'No,' said Adrian, 'there was no sign of that.'

'You know,' I said, 'that's how Winterstein was found too. I could imagine Falk might find that strange, even suspicious. Has the doctor been there?'

'Yes, he's still at Hasselbakken. He also thought the case was peculiar, but couldn't determine any external cause of death. So he concluded, like with Winterstein, that it was heart failure. If it's due to other causes, he said, only an autopsy can reveal them. And he asked me outright whether I believed we should call the police.'

'And what did you say?'

Adrian looked me straight in the eye. 'That the idea was out of the question.'

'So—' I said simply.

'The doctor knew that Arvid Falk is staying here,' Adrian continued. 'And he said it would reassure him to ask Falk what to do. But unfortunately, Falk had been away in Oslo that night. Still, I've notified him, and he's on his way here now. I came down the road in the hope of meeting one of you; the doctor is clearly on the fence.'

Adrian seemed deeply shaken now.

'Suicide?' I asked.

'The doctor considered the possibility,' said Adrian, 'but I don't believe it.'

'Why not?'

'Don't laugh at me,' he burst out suddenly, 'but I'm getting sick of this. I believe there's more going on, things we can't understand! Sacrilege punishes itself. I believe in the Madonna's revenge!'

'Speak,' I said, 'but of course I'm not laughing at you. My dear old friend, this is taking a toll on your nerves. You must, above all, get Jan to leave, so you and Anne Marie can be alone again, so the old days at Hasselbakken can return.'

But Adrian shook his head. 'The old days will never return,' he said.

'But where did you get the idea of the Madonna's revenge?'

'Where?' Adrian was irritated. 'Think of how badly it went for all of us! There were nine of us back then, and now only Jan and I are left.'

'Winterstein died, and his wife and children died; things went wrong for all of us …'

'But not for you,' I blurted out.

'That's just it,' Adrian whispered. 'Now it's my turn.'

'Nonsense,' I said. 'The Madonna has nothing to do with this death; you said yourself that there were no signs of external violence.'

Adrian shook his head. 'Yes, the Madonna *is* involved in this death. It's clear Soten went into Winterstein's room last night before he entered his own. He sat there for a while in front of the Madonna's image and smoked a cigarette; the butt is crushed in the ashtray. He sat there looking at the picture, and the picture looked at him …'

'But people don't just die from looking at a painting,' I said.

A stone rattled on the road; someone was coming. Adrian grabbed my arm and whispered quickly, 'If you're asked your opinion, please do me a favour and say the same.'

'The same?' I repeated, puzzled.

'Yes, that there's nothing behind this death. It won't help anyway. Jan has said the same, and Anne Marie too. But maybe it carries more weight coming from an outsider.'

I didn't get a chance to answer; Arvid Falk came into view. He was warm; he had walked briskly, having just arrived by train. Adrian repeated his account and added that he had left everything untouched in the death room. Falk lit a cigarette and exhaled. He was dressed in sportswear, and he looked hot standing in the blazing sun.

'It could, of course, be a coincidence,' he said, staring absently out over the valley. 'We'll see what we can make of it. As far as I can tell, everyone involved is best served if the matter is handled as discreetly as possible.'

'Absolutely,' said Adrian eagerly. 'There's no reason to involve the police or the public.'

'That depends on the doctor's death certificate,' Falk continued. 'Let's talk to him.'

He began walking up towards Hasselbakken. Along the way, he asked if we'd heard from Bjelke; wasn't he expected to arrive today? Adrian confirmed this. He assumed Bjelke was coming from abroad and would get in touch with Hasselbakken during the day.

'Bjelke …' I said. 'That name seems familiar.'

'You probably have heard it,' Falk replied. 'His name came up quite a bit in connection with a high–profile case some years ago. Bjelke was then a police inspector in Oslo and involved in a case concerning the famous Russian crown diamond, the Orloff. The diamond had gone missing, and a couple of people were killed. It's said Bjelke himself was caught up in the events, though the case was never fully solved. In any case, it resulted in his resignation and his disappearance abroad with a Russian singer. Some claim he took the diamond with him, but that may just be gossip. Anyway, the case was hushed up, and Bjelke left. I've heard she later left him, and that since then he's led something of an adventurous life. At any rate, he should make for an interesting acquaintance.'

Hasselbakken lay bathed in full sunlight. The veranda doors stood open; in the flowerbeds outside, heavy, variegated peonies blazed amidst lush greenery. Violets, velvety auriculas and blue grape hyacinths glowed between the stones. The house seemed nestled in green; only the blue shadows of the trees broke the riot of colour.

Anne Marie and the doctor sat in the drawing room. The doctor had a mineral water in front of him; they were talking about music. When we arrived, they fell silent. Anne Marie must have been crying; her eyes were shiny and damp. Adrian repeated what had happened the previous evening. Tea had been served first—

'Tea?' said the doctor. 'Do you still have the cups?'

We looked questioningly at Anne Marie. She nodded; nothing had been touched.

'But Soten didn't drink,' she said. 'His cup is unused; he didn't want any.'

The doctor looked disappointed. 'Then that won't help us. I had considered that he may have done it voluntarily. Tea is often involved; sleeping powders are often taken in tea, as you know.'

'It may still be of interest,' said Falk. 'If you have any medicine bottles in the house, I'd like to have them rinsed so I can take the residue with me.'

Falk and Anne Marie set about doing this. He rinsed the bottles and took samples, which he labelled and marked. He also took a sample from Soten's untouched cup. Jan had meanwhile joined us. He was serious and pale, and said he too had slept heavily all night and far into the morning. He had heard nothing; it was rare for him to sleep so deeply, he added. Falk also asked about the whisky. There was some left in the bottle, and a couple of glasses stood half–empty. He took samples from these as well.

'Of course, all this may be unnecessary,' said the doctor apologetically. 'But I can't entirely rule out the possibility of suicide. I can't with certainty determine whether this was cardiac arrest. And if it wasn't, then it's my duty to report it to the police.'

'Of course,' said Adrian. 'You must do what your duty requires.'

'That's why it reassures me that Mr. Falk is investigating,' continued the doctor. 'If everything checks out, there's no reason to believe it was anything but heart failure.'

'There's no other way to determine that?' I asked.

The doctor shook his head. 'Not without an autopsy.'

Meanwhile, Falk had finished. We went upstairs; Anne Marie didn't follow us.

Soten lay on the sofa as if asleep. His face, with its sharp, bold lines, was expressionless. A shadow of a smile played across his mouth; not the bitter, grim smile he sometimes wore and which his wild life had etched on his face, but a quiet, inward, almost ironic smile. His head rested on a white pillow and was surrounded by flowers from field and forest; wood anemones, daisies, and lady's slipper orchids. It seemed symbolic. These were not the well–groomed, lush flowers of the garden, but the poor, wild blossoms of bivouac and trench, mountain, forest, and steppe. On his chest lay a small bouquet of violets; a final greeting from the garden at the place where he died.

'Look here,' said Falk suddenly. 'His things are packed.'

This had escaped Adrian's notice. Soten's suitcase was packed and locked. His pyjamas were removed from the made bed – he hadn't used it – and his toiletries were not on the washstand. There was nothing else in the room that drew attention, at least not that I could see. Falk searched high and low. He also went to the window and looked intently at the frame. Then he fetched Soten's keyring and unlocked his suitcase. He didn't seem to find anything noteworthy in there either.

The hallway on the second floor ran at a right angle to the stairs. Straight ahead was the large veranda room where Winterstein had once stayed. To the right of this was Soten's room. There was no door between them; you had to go out into the hallway to enter the other room. Adrian said he had found the door to the veranda room ajar. It had been locked; he was certain of that, since all Winterstein's belongings were inside. He himself kept the key on his own keyring, but, he added, all the keys on the second floor were the same.

'So Soten could have unlocked the veranda room with the key to his own,' Falk observed.

Adrian confirmed this.

'You said he had smoked a cigarette in there,' said Falk. 'How do you know?'

'Because Soten always smoked a particular brand; he had brought a large supply of German cigarettes. And a stub of that brand is in the ashtray in the veranda room.'

We went in. I noticed that Jan was visibly moved again upon seeing the icon; it was no wonder, given what he had endured for it. Falk examined the room thoroughly. An armchair had been pulled out into the middle of the floor, directly in front of the Madonna.

'Was it standing like this when you came in?' Falk asked Adrian.

'Yes.'

Falk said nothing more but continued his examination. He took the cigarette butt carefully between his fingers, noted the brand, then placed it in an envelope and poured the ash into another. He sealed both and put them away with care. He also examined the veranda door very thoroughly. It was locked, and all windows were closed, except the slightly ajar upper tall window, held open by short metal hooks from the inside. It would have been impossible even for an acrobat to squeeze through. Then he went over to the icon.

'The panel was closed when the probate court was here,' said Adrian. 'Soten must have opened it last night.'

Falk looked at the painting for a long time, carefully, from every angle. Then he slowly closed the front panel again.

'I'll show you how it locks,' said Jan. 'You must touch the front around the dove's head …'

'Thank you,' said Falk. 'That's exactly what I wanted to know. We can quickly confirm whether Soten opened the panel last night.'

He examined the golden dove's head closely with a magnifying glass. Then he went into his own room and soon returned with a small case. Falk stopped again in front of the panel and sprinkled some grey, silver–shimmering powder over the little dove's head, brushed it gently with a small brush, and covered it with a piece of film.

'That'll soon do it,' he said contentedly, and placed the film in his wallet. Then he went over to the dead man and took fingerprints.

I had turned to the window while he did all this; the silent figure on the sofa affected me strangely. My part in this whole affair had been minor, and at the start, I may have even behaved more favourably towards Soten's adversary. But through his own account, I had gained an insight into his life as it had unfolded since the days in Olesko; harsh, wild, brutal, barbaric. Should he not be forgiven? He was a mercenary, a man without a country in his time, a wandering soldier of fortune. He belonged to the age of the Thirty Years' War, not ours … Then again, why not precisely in our own desperate time? Have we any reason to judge other eras, to think ourselves better than them?

Down in the garden, Anne Marie walked slowly, her head bowed. She stopped now and then in front of the flowers, adjusting and helping them. Perhaps it was fine just as it was …There was a faint click. Falk had closed the panel; he was finished with his examination. He informed us that he would travel immediately into Oslo to have the samples analysed; he couldn't do it himself.

'That's good,' said the doctor. 'It's urgent; I'd really like to get the death certificate sorted.'

Adrian asked me to stay for dinner; he had an errand down by the station. Jan went with him; they all left in the doctor's car. I went down into the garden. Anne Marie and I sat on a bench, each in our own corner. We didn't have much to say to each other.

'I'll be leaving soon,' I said at last.

'Oh?' she replied simply. 'I understand,' she added.

'How little we know our own future,' she continued suddenly. 'Come, sit closer; let's talk for a moment like in the old days. How little we knew what lay ahead of us that evening at Hasselbakken, when we sat in front of the fireplace and I was a little … a little harsh with Adrian; when I wished that we, too, could take part in the wild upheaval constantly happening in the world. You thought I was being unreasonable, I could tell.'

I protested, said of course I could understand her, but that on the other hand …

'Yes, deep down you thought I was being awkward,' she insisted. 'But you didn't believe I meant it; you took it as a romantic fancy. But it wasn't, don't you see? People want to live through their own time, whether it's good or bad, whether it brings sunshine or storm. But still, we have our weak moments.'

Her voice suddenly broke. 'Because it's terrible,' she continued quietly. 'It's so unreal and frightening; we're caught up in some raging current, and we can't fight against it. Every day things happen that I can't understand. Why did Kunz Soten die? Why did he come through a thousand dangers only to perish here?'

I didn't answer; what was I supposed to say?

'One day it'll all be over,' I said at last. 'And we'll return to the old, safe, peaceful life at Hasselbakken.'

'No!' she cried. 'No, that will never return, and I'm glad!'

She looked at me, and there was a hostile expression in her tear-filled eyes. I looked away, and again minutes passed in silence. We sat deep in our own thoughts. The wind played with her hair; I could see it from the side.

'Did you like him?' she suddenly asked.

I hesitated. ' …in a way …' I said evasively.

Anne Marie suddenly sobbed; she pulled out her handkerchief and bowed her head. I could see from her shoulders that she was crying quietly.

'There was so much good in him,' she said.

'There's good in all people, Anne Marie,' I said. 'But do you really think he belonged in our part of the world?'

She didn't answer.

Some time later, Adrian and Jan returned. Dinner was strained. To lighten the mood, I spoke of Bjelke, whom we were expecting; I simply repeated what Falk had told me about him. I added a touch sarcastically that he was a man whose colourful past could rival the standard at Hasselbakken.

That afternoon, Soten was taken to the chapel and shortly after, Bjelke phoned to announce his arrival that same evening. Things were moving along; perhaps in a few days the icon would be out of the house, Jan would be gone, and everything would be in order. Anne Marie would surely find peace again; maybe we could finally go on that mountain trip we'd so often talked about. It would do us all good. I cautiously began bringing it up, but I was interrupted by Falk's arrival. He was full of energy and buzzing with news.

'How did you sleep last night?' he asked Anne Marie.

'Heavily,' she replied. 'Terribly heavily. And I've been drowsy all day, even with everything that's happened. Must be the weather.'

'Do you ever take sleeping pills, madam?'

'No,' she said. 'Very rarely.'

'How do they usually affect you?'

'I get heavy in the head,' she said. 'I sleep deeply, dreamlessly, and I'm tired the next day; yes, exactly like today.'

Falk turned to Adrian and Jan. They confirmed that they too had slept deeply.

'So you all drank tea?' he asked.

'Well,' he continued, 'my investigations haven't been entirely in vain. The whisky was fine, but all the tea remnants showed a strong dose of a commonly used sleeping drug!'

We looked at each other.

'A strong dose?' I repeated. 'Do you mean it could have been fatal?'

'No,' said Falk, 'but it was about double the usual dose. The mix was strong enough that anyone who drank the tea would definitely fall into a deep sleep, and not wake up from someone moving around … or, say, leaving the house.'

He paused, then added: 'Now the question is: Who mixed the drug into the tea? And who had the opportunity?'

'I must declare myself entirely innocent,' said Anne Marie with a faint smile. 'I suppose I'm suspect, since I made the tea, but I am still innocent.'

'Where did you make it?'

'In the kitchen.'

'Did you bring it in immediately?'

'No, I let it steep for a while.'

'Could anyone have had free access to the kitchen during that time?'

'I don't know; I went into the drawing room to sit down. But everyone in the house naturally had access to the kitchen; we were in and out.'

'And you're sure Soten didn't touch his cup?'

'Yes, that's why Adrian brought out the whisky.'

Falk settled comfortably into an armchair and leaned back, exhaling his cigarette smoke in large, steady rings.

'My next bit of news,' he said offhandedly – it was clear he enjoyed his role – 'is that the fingerprints on the panel match Soten's! We can now reconstruct the events with high certainty. Soten gains access to the kitchen and pours a heavy dose of sleeping medicine into the teapot. This dose is strong enough that he can count on everyone who drinks the tea falling into a deep sleep, without being disturbed if someone moves around or leaves the house. He refuses to drink it himself; an important point because he knows that the next day he might be suspected of having tampered with the tea. He can't be entirely sure of the effect; perhaps you would all sleep late and grow suspicious. Even if no one else suspected him, I believe his comrade, Mr Jan, would have.

'But this shows one thing: Soten didn't take that risk seriously. He had no intention of returning; he meant to disappear. He had already packed his suitcase and prepared everything for departure. Soten calmly waits while the rest of you go to bed. He perhaps packs his things then goes into the veranda room, pulls a chair into the middle of the floor, opens the panel, lights a cigarette, and sits there in peace and quiet, admiring the icon. But perhaps he begins to feel unwell. He goes into his room, lies down for a moment, and in that short instant, fate catches up with him, and he dies.'

'Of heart failure?' asked Adrian.

Falk shrugged.

CHAPTER XI

The doctor nevertheless issued a death certificate for Soten the same day. Falk had spoken with him, then phoned us with the news. What Falk had said, or how he managed to persuade the doctor to do it, I don't know. Besides, there was nothing that indicated that Soten had died in any unnatural way. If Falk's theory was correct, Soten had intended to leave; perhaps he had wanted to take the icon with him, and possibly he had secured his retreat by mixing a sleeping agent into the tea. But that was all we knew. In the middle of his preparations, his heart had failed; such things can happen. If the death made such a grim impression on us, it was probably due to our nerves and the fact that Winterstein had died in the same manner.

For our nerves *were* on edge; the old war stories loomed near again because the main characters had acted them out and reminisced before our eyes. Perhaps religious notions also played a part, as generations of inherited fear of sacrilege and careful centuries–old precautions from the clergy still made themselves felt; it was, of course, our nerves … I pointed this out to Adrian and Anne Marie while we waited. Falk was to meet Bjelke at the station and show him the way; we wouldn't expect them before half past seven. Time passed slowly; outside, it was still light, but the last sunshine played over the treetops.

Then we finally heard footsteps coming up the hill and Falk came into view. At his side walked a medium–height, slender man in light summer clothing. He stopped in front of the veranda and took a quick look over the house; at that moment I saw his face. It was regular and rather handsome; several fine, nervous lines showed that life had not passed over it without a trace, and the hair at his temples was lightly greying. I estimated his age to lie somewhere between thirty and forty. He greeted us with a faint smile and was immediately introduced before any of us had said anything.

'Mrs Krebs; Mr Krebs, I presume,' he said and bowed, 'and this gentleman—' he switched to German, '—must be the Pauliner monk Brother Jan … and then – Herr Müller from *Heilige Lampe*, I assume?'

'My real name is Wiig,' I said, annoyed. Anne Marie gave me a quick glance. Bjelke was impressively well–informed.

'It is perhaps rather unconventional,' he continued, 'that I must at once request a private conversation with Brother Jan. Let it serve as my excuse that my visit is chiefly a business matter.'

'Of course,' said Adrian, somewhat surprised, 'the drawing room is at your disposal.'

'I haven't told him anything about the recent events,' said Falk quickly once we were alone, 'he seemed to be very well–informed, however; who knows where he could have been tipped off!'

'But the singer?' asked Anne Marie suddenly, 'the singer for whose sake he lost his position; what became of her?'

'I don't know,' said Falk, 'I've only seen in the papers that she is currently giving concerts in America, and I once heard a rumour that it was over between them, and that Bjelke had completely broken down and sought work as an international spy. But he doesn't seem down in any way.' 'You can tell he's been through a lot,' said Anne Marie, 'he has an interesting face.

'What became of the diamond?'

'She probably kept it,' replied Falk, 'in any case, I know nothing about it.'

'I'll ask him about it,' said Anne Marie, and for a moment used her old, carefree tone, then she became serious again and added with a furrowed brow:

'By the way, I like his story, I like people who can stake everything on a single great moment; that's probably what he did then. But he doesn't look like someone who regrets it. One never really regrets what one had to do because one had the courage to do it.'

What she meant by this, I don't know, for Bjelke and Jan came back in just then; their conversation had only lasted a few minutes.

We sat down out on the veranda. Anne Marie served tea and sandwiches. Bjelke said a few words about the view; we could get to the point, but no one said anything yet. It was Bjelke who began. 'I hear that Winterstein is dead,' he said without addressing anyone in particular.

'Yes,' replied Adrian, 'it's been a while now, but you may not know we had a fresh tragedy yesterday: Kunz Soten died.'

Bjelke's face abruptly changed expression. It became hard and contorted; a pair of vertical furrows appeared in his forehead and cut sharply across the small nervous lines running across it. His eyes became cold and alert.

'I didn't know that,' he said shortly, 'but I would greatly appreciate hearing the full details.'

'Better that Mr Falk tells it,' said Adrian, biting the tip off a cigar.

Falk recounted in brief what had happened, and Bjelke now and then interjected with a few questions; it seemed he knew the background of the case well. He also asked to be given all the details regarding Winterstein's death. He took out a notebook and jotted down a few things. Then he asked to see the photographs from the night of the break–in. Falk took them out of his wallet, and Bjelke studied them for a long time attentively, even asking to borrow a magnifying glass.

'Yes, you are aware these pictures were taken?' he finally asked, addressing Jan.

Jan smiled politely and made an apologetic gesture. 'We had to give it a try,' he said calmly, as if the fact that he had tried to break in to steal an icon was the most ordinary thing in the world.

'Soten and I intended to get hold of the Madonna, but we had to give up when the alarm went off. I naturally didn't know I'd been photographed; I have, for that matter, seen the pictures once before,' he added. 'Winterstein showed them to me.'

'Winterstein?' repeated Bjelke.

Jan blew the cigarette smoke out in large, even, blue–grey rings and followed them attentively with his eyes as they drifted under the veranda roof.

'Yes,' he said indifferently. 'We made a kind of truce before he, unfortunately, passed away.'

Bjelke looked quickly at him, but said nothing. Instead, he turned to Falk and asked to see the fingerprints he had taken from Soten. These too he examined for a long time through the magnifying glass, and his brow was once again furrowed; it appeared he was intensely working through the problem. Then he asked to see the icon and added that he would greatly appreciate if Falk could demonstrate what Soten had presumably done after the others had gone to bed.

We all followed. First we went to Soten's room. Everything was as before, except that Soten had been taken away. Falk showed how the body had been lying when we found it.

'In the old days,' said Bjelke, 'when I was still in the police, I had a couple of friends I often killed time with. One was a promising young doctor – he's since become a professor – and the other was a well–known divorce lawyer. We occasionally made mutual use of each other's experience. One of the doctor's theories was that every year there are many poison murders in this country which are never discovered. It occurs especially in unhappy marriages;

the husband or wife is found dead one day without any visible injuries, and the doctor, who usually knows the family, willingly issues a death certificate.

Naturally, you can't blame him for doing so when there are no specific clues; if he refused, it would amount to an unheard–of accusation, yes, a direct charge. So it's not the doctor's fault, but the law's. It ought to be mandatory that the cause of death is always determined, even if it requires an autopsy; that was what my doctor friend claimed. He used to tease the lawyer by saying that he was the one who missed out on such cases, either as a divorce lawyer or as a defence attorney. He said that in this way he lost out twice over: first the divorce, since the troublesome party had simply been gotten rid of, and then the murder case, since the guilty party got away scot–free.'

'In this case, then, the deceased was immediately brought to the chapel with the doctor's permission?'

Adrian nodded. 'He said explicitly that he felt reassured that Falk was taking care of the matter.'

Bjelke looked around. 'The water glass, was it examined?'

'It was clean and contained no residue,' answered Falk.

'It may have been rinsed,' said Bjelke, 'and residues evaporate easily in this weather. But let's move on.'

The veranda room was also untouched; Bjelke looked around with interest.

'So here Soten sat and smoked a cigarette while he looked at the icon,' said Falk, pointing. 'Perhaps he waited to be sure the others were sound asleep.'

'Did Soten have anything to light it with?' asked Bjelke suddenly.

We looked at each other somewhat uncertainly; none of us had noticed whether he had used anything.

'Yes, because you didn't mention finding any matches in the ashtray; so he must have had his cigarette lit when he entered.'

'That probably doesn't matter much,' said Falk.

'Perhaps not,' said Bjelke. 'But it's possible he simply crushed the cigarette in the ashtray. You can easily tell from the amount of ash that you found.'

Falk didn't answer this; he had gone over to the icon.

'How does one open it?' he asked Jan.

The monk stood over by the window with his back to us. He turned slowly; his face was in shadow.

'Grasp the dove's head and turn it slowly to the right,' he answered. 'When it lies completely back with the beak pointing straight up, you will hear a click and the panel is open.'

Bjelke instinctively took a step forward, the panel opened, and the icon appeared glowing through the dusk in a radiant, otherworldly blue. Jan bowed by the window and made the sign of the cross quietly. Bjelke was deeply moved.

'I can understand Winterstein better now, after having seen it,' he said quietly.

We were silent for a while, and when we began speaking again, our voices were instinctively lowered, like in a church. Then Falk closed the panel again and we returned to the veranda. Adrian set out whisky and soda.

'That was an experience,' said Bjelke; we were still caught up in the reverent mood.

The summer night added to it. It lay like soft velvet over forest and fields; the garden's white peonies glowed through the twilight, and a gentle, monotonous rustling came from the woods. Adrian broke the silence.

'You are astonishingly well–informed about all of it,' he said.

'Yes,' answered Bjelke openly, 'I know the gist of the events in Olesko, and I also know the history of the icon.'

Anne Marie joined in and asked him to recount it.

'She is sometimes called the Madonna of Vengeance,' began Bjelke.

'We've heard that,' said Anne Marie eagerly, 'but I don't remember who told us.'

'It was Winterstein,' I said, 'who repeated the monk's last words on the threshold in Olesko.'

We all looked at Jan; he nodded calmly.

'I also know the history of the icon,' he said.

At that moment Anne Marie dropped her shawl, and Jan picked it up. I noticed that he was careful, almost tender, in his movement as he laid it over her shoulders.

'Legend has it that the painting was made by Saint Luke,' said Bjelke. 'Luke painted two images, the Blue Madonna and the Black Madonna; both remained in Jerusalem until the fourth century after Christ. Then the Empress Helena, mother of Constantine the Great, made a pilgrimage to Jerusalem and received the two paintings as a gift from the city's Jewish women. In Constantine's treasury, the paintings lay for half a millennium and eventually ended up at the castle of Belz in Galicia. But when the Tatars invaded the land in 1382, Duke Vladislaus Jagello removed his treasures from the castle and divided them equally among the faiths.

'He sent the Black Madonna to the Roman Catholic hermit monastery in Częstochowa and the Blue Madonna to the Greek Catholic monastery in Borodjanka. The Black Madonna arrived safely at Jasna Góra, while the Blue Madonna fell into the hands of the Tatars just outside the monastery walls. Now the legend tells that the Tatar leader, a few weeks later, sent word to the monastery and humbly asked whether they would accept the painting, as it was deadly, and his men were dying in large numbers in front of it.

'Thus the painting was safely returned. A similar story comes from the time of Mazepa. His Cossacks occupied the monastery, and a band of them took the icon with them as they moved on. But death ravaged them, and when the rumour spread, the monks set off and offered to deliver them from the plague if they would atone and return the Madonna. On that occasion too, it is said that the Cossacks died in front of it. A third story also comes to mind. A well–known robber in Ukraine who feared neither Heaven nor Hell had sworn that he would break into the monastery and steal the image of the Mother of God.

'Somehow he succeeded, but he was found dead in front of the altar … It is, as I said, all legend. Perhaps legends created with the deliberate intention of spreading fear and protecting the treasures of the monasteries; but it's certainly true that the ordinary monks and local population believe just as firmly in the Madonna's ability to take a terrible and mysterious revenge as in her power to perform miraculous deeds.'

'But the story persists even in our sceptical days,' said Adrian in a broken voice; it came like a groan through the twilight. 'From Olesko to here, there have been death upon death and misfortune upon misfortune. In just the last ten days, two bodies have lain at the feet of the Madonna …'

Bjelke was about to respond, but Jan's voice interrupted him:

'It says in the book of Ecclesiastes,' he said: 'Then I praised the dead who are already dead more than the living who are still alive. But better than both is the one who has not yet been, who has not seen the evil work that is done under the sun'.'

His tone was ambiguous; it was impossible to tell whether he spoke the words in deadly seriousness or if they were merely meant as an apt quotation. I could just make out a cool, detached smile that passed over his face. It was like a voice from another time, far away and unreal; and again, there was silence among us. We sat there each in our own chair, in our own world.

'My belief is,' I finally said, attempting to imitate Jan's tone that still seemed to linger in the air, 'that it can all be explained as a mixture of coincidence and an intense form of mass psychosis. We don't need to bother with the old legend; we can allow ourselves to doubt whether these events really took place. But on the other hand, it's perhaps not unnatural for complexes to arise among those who commit such acts, especially as this icon alone, as a work of art, affects people so powerfully. Also consider the ideas of sacrilege that have been passed down through generations.

'When, then, the involved parties hear mysterious tales of the vengeance the icon is said to take, it's only natural that everything tends toward certain misfortunes actually happening. That all this condensed in Soten at the very moment he tried to seize the Madonna and saw it before him, we may well assume. And that this may have affected a heart which perhaps was already weak; that is also not entirely improbable.'

But the words rang hollow, and I didn't believe them myself.

Bjelke suddenly began to speak in a loud voice; it was as if he felt compelled to break the mood that hung over us.

'I must say I agree with my old friend, the professor,' he said, 'that in such cases, one absolutely must determine the cause of death. There are, after all, many possibilities here.'

'Yes, for example?' I asked.

Bjelke looked straight ahead and did not answer directly. 'Who can know whether the sleeping agent was present in all the cups beforehand,' he said curtly. 'It's not my place to interfere in this. But suppose Soten acted with someone else, and that this someone killed him and afterwards poured the sleeping agent into one or more cups—'

Jan laughed quietly. 'You think it was murder,' he said. 'What motives could there be, and who would have done it? And how?'

'As I said, it's not my place to interfere,' said Bjelke. 'But I have previously experienced a case where old superstition was exploited. And that time, it led to murder!'

A chill crept over the veranda. It had grown dark outside; a blinding white flash of light suddenly burst violently in the curve of the road above the church and set a glowing strip across the landscape. We saw the outline of the forest for a moment.

Bjelke looked at his watch. 'It's late,' he said. 'I'd like to return to Oslo tonight. When is the next train?'

It was in half an hour; he said he'd like to take one more look at Soten's room. Anne Marie and I followed him up, and she switched on the light.

'There, look,' he said, immediately pointing to the ashtray, 'there's a burnt–out match and a good bit of ash; he must have lit the cigarette in here …'

He suddenly fell silent and stared at something; I followed the direction of his gaze. On the nightstand stood a match container. Bjelke picked it up and looked at it for a long time.

'It's a brand–new box of matches,' he said. 'The striking surface has only been used once. I wonder when this box of matches was placed here?'

'I can tell you that,' said Anne Marie. 'I put it there myself; Soten smoked a lot and had used up the previous box. I put a new one there after lunch before … yes, before …'

'That's very interesting,' I heard him mutter. 'It might explain things.'

We said our goodbyes out on the veranda. I was heading the same way and offered to walk Bjelke to the station. Falk also intended to leave, but Adrian begged him earnestly to stay.

'We'll meet tomorrow anyway,' said Bjelke. 'You'll come to see me at my hotel, won't you?'

Falk promised he would.

'By the way,' said Bjelke, as if something had just occurred to him, 'I'd like to look again at the fingerprints. Would you mind lending them to me? May I keep them until tomorrow?'

He was given them and immediately went into the living room where there was light, and studied them again, then slipped them into his inside pocket and declared himself ready to leave. When we had come down the hill, he turned and called loudly up to the veranda:

'I'll stop by the Probate Court tomorrow and present my credentials; I have my authorisation in order and assume the entire matter can be settled quickly. As soon as all the formalities are clarified, I'll come out and collect Winterstein's belongings, also the icon, the Blue Madonna!'

'All right,' I heard Adrian reply. 'And you'll be most welcome.'

'Whom do you actually represent in this matter?' I asked when we had walked a bit further down the road.

'The Pauline Order,' Bjelke answered. 'And I also have the consent of the heirs.'

We walked on a while in silence. Soten's death would not leave my thoughts; so much had been said and implied that evening.

'You were the one who went to Cologne on Krebs' behalf?' Bjelke suddenly asked.

I confirmed it, and a half–forgotten incident instantly came back to me.

'How strange,' I said. 'Do you know that when I returned, my friend Adrian said something to me that has now fully come true. It was when I told him about the meeting between Winterstein, Soten, and Jan. He said: "Those three will chase each other to death …"

I regretted it as soon as the words left me.

'Is that so,' said Bjelke slowly, 'so he already knew then that the three of them would chase each other to death … He's nearly been proven right. What has taken place here is, all in all, not difficult to understand; the evidence seems obvious. But, as I've said, it's simply not my business.'

It was the third time that evening he emphasised that it was not his affair.

The next day, it was still sunny. I spent the day in a deckchair, had the occasional drink, and sometimes used my binoculars. I saw nothing of Bjelke or Adrian, and no one phoned me. In the evening, I went into Oslo and met up with my drinking companion from a few days earlier. We shared a bottle of whisky.

The following day was heavy and grey, and my head ached. Dark banks of cloud drifted overhead, and the air was humid and oppressive. It was the third of July; I remember the day because that was when the rainy period set in, which lasted the rest of the month. And it was then that events moved the Hasselbakken affair from the realm of strange and adventurous to the sober and prosaic realm of criminal investigation.

In what follows, I shall let the facts speak for themselves, even more so because I was mentioned in the case as a witness. I will therefore quote the police's official report on the murder at Hasselbakken. The report is essentially a summary of the case, and to make the overview easier, I have omitted a good number of irrelevant details.

CHAPTER XII

Document 1 – Report.
On 8 July at 1:55 a.m., the sheriff telephoned the local police station and requested immediate assistance as that a dead man, allegedly killed by several gunshots, had been found at Villa Hasselbakken. The sheriff gave directions, stating they should drive as far as Smedsvingen, where he would send his constable to guide them further. Police Superintendent Vang was immediately notified by telephone. He gave orders to alert Detective Officer I. Karlsen to report to the station within twenty minutes.

Respectfully,

F. Jensen, Police Constable

Document 2 – Report from Police Superintendent Vang.
At 2:55 a.m., the undersigned and Detective Officer Karlsen arrived at Villa Hasselbakken, where a murdered man was allegedly discovered that night. Present at the villa upon our arrival were the owner, musician Adrian Krebs and his wife, who had made the discovery upon returning from Oslo that same night, along with the sheriff and his constable, and a friend of the household, law graduate Arvid Falk, who is currently residing there. It was stated that the deceased was a Polish citizen named Jan Kurzcpetowski. He had been staying as a guest in the house for the past month.

The further circumstances were as follows:

Krebs and his wife had taken the 5:00 p.m. train that day into Oslo, where they attended the premiere of the opera *Orpheus*. Krebs, who is employed in the orchestra, had played the harp. After the performance, the couple, along with Falk and a neighbour named Valdemar Wiig, had stayed at a restaurant until all four took the midnight train back. At the station, they parted with Wiig, and upon arrival at the house, they immediately sensed something was wrong as the front door stood open. Upon entering the living room, they found the Pole lying dead on the floor. Krebs immediately notified the sheriff and a doctor. The latter arrived and confirmed that the deceased had died as a result of three gunshot wounds inflicted at close range. The doctor was later called out on a medical visit but was to return.

Those present assured us that nothing had been disturbed at the scene; the doctor had examined the deceased without changing the position of the body. I requested that the parties move into a side room while we conducted our investigation. Mr Falk remained present during these.

The house is a two–storey villa in modernised Swiss style. There are three entrances to the house: the main door at the back, the kitchen door on the north side of the house, which lies east–west, and finally, the veranda door on the east side. The latter door is usually used in summer and normally left open.

Upon the family's return that night, however, they found this door closed and locked from the inside. The main door, on the other hand, was open. It is therefore likely that the perpetrator or perpetrators entered this way and also left through it. Inside the door is a small entryway that serves as a kind of vestibule. Beyond this lies the hall, from which doors lead into the various rooms. The door between the hall and the living room was also open, according to Mr Krebs. I refer otherwise to the attached diagram, Appendix 1. The living room is five by six metres and has two windows: namely, the veranda door and a narrower window to the left (north) of the door – see diagram.

In the middle of the floor lay the deceased, face down in a pool of blood. He was already cold, and rigor mortis had begun to set in.

The blood was almost congealed. We photographed the body and marked it on the diagram. Before we touched it, we searched everywhere for fingerprints, including the door handle and a glass on the table. We also preserved the contents of this glass, which appeared to be half–filled with water. We found several usable fingerprints, but whether these belong to the perpetrator(s) will be the subject of further investigation. On the carpet, we also found some hairs, which we preserved.

The deceased had presumably been reading the evening newspaper when the perpetrator entered. That day's paper was spread out on the sofa. At my request, the sheriff explained that the evening papers were delivered by courier. I asked him to ensure a statement was obtained from the newspaper delivery boy. Krebs explained, when asked, that the deceased often read Norwegian newspapers to try to learn the language.

No cartridge casings were found. However, one bullet had gone through the left side pane of the veranda door at a height of 113 cm from the floor. We photographed the hole in the glass and followed the trajectory out onto the veranda. There, we found that the bullet had embedded itself in one of the veranda posts. With a knife, we were able to extract it. It was a lead bullet, calibre .32 or .320.

From this, and from the fact that no casings were found, I conclude that the weapon used was not a pistol, but a revolver of the said calibre. That this is a case of murder is evident from the absence of any weapon at the scene and from the fact that, according to the doctor, the body was struck by three bullets.

While awaiting the doctor's return, we continued our investigation of the adjacent rooms. Out in the hallway, an important find was made: namely, a crumpled lace–edged lady's handkerchief. I showed this to Mrs Krebs, who stated that it did not belong to her and that she had never seen it before. She was also the one who pointed out the lace edging.

Further investigations outside the house revealed the print of a high-heeled woman's shoe leading away from the house. The imprint was clear. There were also several prints from a different type of woman's shoe. We made plaster casts of all the tracks, including the boot prints. By comparing them on-site, we could confirm that the first print came from a shoe somewhat larger than those worn by Mrs Krebs.

The lady stated that she had a housemaid. To be sure, the sheriff's constable was immediately dispatched to obtain the maid's shoes, and he returned with them. As they were of a completely different type and size, we contented ourselves with photographing them before sending them back. (The newspaper delivery boy is around 15 years old – his tracks are not relevant in this context.)

The doctor had now arrived, and we proceeded to examine the body. It had been struck by three bullets – one in the right shoulder and two in the left side of the chest. I omit the details here, as they will appear in the autopsy report. With the aid of a magnifying glass, we were able to detect gunpowder grains in the fabric around one of the chest wounds and conclude that at least this shot had been fired at close range. The shoulder wound also showed an exit hole on the back beneath the shoulder blade.

By searching in the likely direction, we found in a corner of the room a flattened lead bullet. No impact mark on the wall could be found, despite careful examination, and it is therefore possible that the bullet was flattened against the shoulder blade and exited sideways. The autopsy will, however, bring certainty on this point.

From the position of the body and the bullet wounds, it seems reasonable to conclude that the deceased had been standing in the middle of the floor facing the door when the fatal shots were fired – possibly he charged at the perpetrator, with the result that the final shot was fired at very close range. The perpetrator presumably stood near the door. There is no sign that he or she – or they – remained in the room for any length of time. Apart from the glass of water, which may have been used by the deceased himself, there were no other glasses or plates set out, and in the ashtray there were only three cigarette stubs of the same brand found in the deceased's case. Nothing therefore suggests that this was a rendezvous or romantic adventure on the part of the deceased in his host's absence.

With this, we concluded the investigation of the scene and proceeded to gather information about the deceased and to question those present. The sheriff, in the meantime, began an inventory of the deceased's possessions – see Appendix 2.

Inside the inner pocket of the deceased was a Mauser pistol, calibre 7.65 – the weapon had one cartridge in the chamber and four in the magazine. He appears to have entered Norway on 11 June this year and had legally reported his stay. He arrived together with a German friend named Kunz Soten. This man died at Hasselbakken just under a week ago, according to the death certificate, from heart failure. The purpose of the stay in Norway is said to have been to resolve a dispute concerning an icon which the deceased, together with some comrades, is believed to have brought from the occupied territories during the war. The dispute is said to have been settled on the basis that all parties agreed to return the icon to its rightful owners, namely the Pauline Order in Poland. Former Police Superintendent Finn Bjelke has recently arrived in the country with a mandate from the said order.

Krebs states that the deceased's Norwegian acquaintances, as far as he knows, are limited to himself and his wife, Bjelke, Falk, and Wiig. He has never heard him mention any others. Krebs could not imagine any motive for the crime, or how it might have occurred. A full report of the witness interrogations was taken by Detective

Officer Karlsen. However, the interrogation of Mrs Krebs is still outstanding, as she was severely affected by the events and received a sleeping draught from the doctor. Following a preliminary examination, the doctor believes he can determine that Jan K. had been dead for 6 to 8 hours. The murder must therefore have taken place between 5:30 p.m. and 7:30 p.m. on the 7th of the current month.

Among the deceased's papers was found a letter in Latin addressed to him and sealed with the seal of the Pauline Order. With combined effort, we succeeded in deciphering its meaning. The deceased was given the opportunity—contrary to all rules—to re–enter the monastery at Mons Clarus (in parentheses noted: Jasna Góra in Poland) before 1 October of the same year, in consideration of the special merits he had acquired. The letter is attached as Appendix 3. It is dated 27 June. As it did not appear possible to obtain further information at the scene as to who the perpetrator might be, the investigation was provisionally suspended at 7:30 a.m., after I had by telephone arranged for the necessary measures to continue it.

Respectfully,
Hans Vang

Appendices:
1. Sketch
2. Inventory of the deceased's belongings
3. Letter from the Pauline Order dated 27 June 1935
4. Passport with the deceased's personal details
5–14. Envelopes containing evidence from the crime scene
15. Handkerchief found in the hallway
16–23. Plaster casts of footprints
24. Lead bullet found in veranda post
25. Lead bullet found in the living room
26–32. Photographs

Document 3 – Report from Detective Officer Karlsen.
According to orders from Police Superintendent Vang, the undersigned has interrogated the individuals with whom the deceased had contact during his stay in Norway. Common to all witnesses is that none of them can imagine why or how the murder was committed, nor do they have any suspicion against specific persons as the perpetrator.

On the night of 8 July, the following were interrogated at Hasselbakken:
Adrian Krebs, musician, 38 years old, etc. He states:

The deceased, whom we all simply called Jan, I met briefly many years ago during the war. He arrived with a German named Kunz Soten in early July. During the last three weeks, he has stayed with us at Hasselbakken. Yesterday I was to play harp during the premiere of Gluck's *Orpheus*, and had to travel into town for a final rehearsal with the 5 p.m. train. My wife travelled with me, while the deceased stayed behind at Hasselbakken. I asked him if he wanted to join us, but he declined; why, I don't know. The train takes half an hour into Oslo, and I went straight to the theatre where I arrived in good time for the rehearsal, which began at 6 p.m. My wife was going to the hairdresser, and we parted at the West Railway Station. The rehearsal lasted about three–quarters of an hour, but I remained for a while with some colleagues until I met my wife at 7:30 p.m. at the Atheneum. Together we went to the Theatre Café where, as agreed, we met Valdemar Wiig, who was also attending the premiere. My wife and I arrived a little late for the appointment; we sat together until it was nearly eight, then I went to the orchestra while my wife and Wiig went into the theatre. The performance lasted until 10:45 p.m. Afterwards we met again, and Arvid Falk joined us. We went to the same restaurant and remained there until we had to catch the midnight train. The colleagues I sat with after the rehearsal were the cellist Werner and the violinist Gran. The porter at the café can confirm that we were there from 7:30 until nearly 8 p.m. and after the end of the performance.

Read aloud and approved,

Adrian Krebs (signed)

Arvid Falk, law graduate, 30 years old, proprietor of a legal bureau, etc. He states:

I remained at my office yesterday from 4 p.m. until nearly 8 p.m., as I was engaged in a case and had several meetings. My secretary can confirm this. Afterwards I was at the *Orpheus* premiere from just before it began until it ended. I sat next to lawyer K. and his wife, whom I know, and they can confirm this. During the intermission, I greeted Mrs Krebs and Wiig; I had tried to greet them earlier, but they did not recognise me in the dark. After the performance, I met them as agreed, and we went to a restaurant. We then all took the train back together, as I have for some time been staying out at Hasselbakken with them.

Read aloud and approved,

Arvid Falk

The next day I interrogated **Valdemar Wiig**, 33 years old, private gentleman, etc. He states:

I travelled in with the 6 p.m. train and arrived in Oslo at 6:30. I stopped to buy some cigarettes, then went straight to the Theatre Café, where I was to meet Krebs and his wife, but they only arrived at 7:30, so I passed the time reading the newspapers. We sat together until we went into the theatre. I was present for the entire performance, which can be confirmed by Captain B., who sat on the same bench and with whom I exchanged a few words during each intermission. Afterwards I went with Krebs, his wife and Falk to a restaurant, where we stayed until we all took the train home. Otherwise, I know nothing about the case. The conductor on the 6 p.m. train can confirm that I travelled to Oslo, as I had forgotten my season ticket and had to purchase a ticket onboard.

Read aloud and approved,
Valdemar Wiig

Anne Marie Krebs, 27 years old, wife of Adrian Krebs
She gave a statement entirely consistent with her husband's, whose account was read aloud to her and accepted as her own.

Finn Bjelke, former police superintendent, 37 years old – He states:
I am in Norway on a special assignment from the Greek–Catholic Pauline Order to retrieve an icon which was removed from a Russian monastery during the war. The icon had ended up here in Norway in the possession of a certain Winterstein, whose estate has held it. I have also secured permission from Winterstein's sole heir for the icon to be handed over to me. Two days ago, all formalities were in order, and I travelled out to Hasselbakken to collect the icon. I knew the deceased only briefly and had only been with him a few times. On 7 July, I had dinner at a café and afterwards went to my hotel to rest. I believe I rested between 5:00 p.m. and 6:00 p.m. Then I got dressed and went to a bar where I was to meet an old acquaintance of mine, Professor Heim. He arrived at 6:30 p.m., and we were together through the evening, parting only around 1 a.m. When I'm not otherwise engaged, I always dine at the same café, and the waiter might be able to confirm that I was there that day. I believe the lift boy may recall that I, as stated, returned to the hotel. I didn't see the porter and had to take my own key from the rack.

Read aloud and approved,
Finn Bjelke

After consulting with the police superintendent, I verified these alibis, as these individuals are the only ones known to have had contact with the deceased.

Musicians Werner and Gran confirmed that Krebs, between 6:45 p.m. and 7:20 p.m., was in their company at the theatre, and likewise that he was present at the rehearsal from 6:00 p.m. to 6:45 p.m. and performed during the evening's show. Mrs Krebs' presence at the hairdresser between 6:00 p.m. and 7:15 p.m. is also verified. The waiter at the restaurant 'Teaterkaféen' confirmed that Wiig had sat there for quite some time waiting for Krebs and his wife; he had served him two drinks and provided several illustrated magazines. He also remembered that the four of them came in after the performance and remained until just before the café closed. Falk's secretary and lawyer K. confirmed his statement, and Captain B. confirmed that Wiig had sat in the theatre throughout the performance with a lady, with whom he exchanged a few words during each intermission. The conductor remembered that Wiig had bought a ticket on the 6:00 p.m. train, as he was a regular traveller. Professor Heim had been with Bjelke during the time in question, and the waiter Bjelke mentioned remembered serving him on 7 July. The lift boy was less certain – 'he thought he might recall taking him up in the lift, but whether it was on the 6th or 7th, he couldn't say for sure'.

Respectfully,
Jens Karlsen

Document 5.
Telegram from Polizeidirektion Magdeburg (translated):
Eva Mendel, employed at firm Magdeburg, confirmed to have stayed here on 7 July. Stop.

Document 6.
Report from Detective Officer Karlsen:

According to instructions from Superintendent Vang, the undersigned has conducted investigations concerning how the perpetrator may have reached Hasselbakken, with special attention paid to the possibility that the perpetrator could have been a woman. The district sheriff was instructed to cooperate with me, working under the theory that the crime might have been committed by a local man or woman.

From the sheriff's report, it is clear that he immediately examined the muddy driveway for any possible tyre tracks when he was called. Only one vehicle had driven up before his own—the doctor's. But the road is so narrow that one must constantly adjust the steering, so it is unavoidable that tracks from a foreign vehicle would have been visible, as the doctor's would have crossed over them. The sheriff therefore considers it impossible that a foreign vehicle had driven up to Hasselbakken that evening, though one could certainly have waited on the main road.

Further, it was reported that the newspaper boy rang the bell and delivered the newspaper precisely at 6:00 p.m. that evening. The deceased opened the door for him and thanked him in broken Norwegian. The delivery boy is likely the last person to have seen him alive.

I have examined three possibilities regarding the murderess's route to and from the scene: train, car, and bus. Trains that could be relevant include those departing at 6:15 p.m. and 7:15 p.m., and the return at 7:00 p.m., assuming the killer left immediately after the crime. None of the conductors had noticed anything unusual; I also spoke with conductors on other trains, but none could provide information. There are usually many local passengers, and since we cannot provide a description, the question was narrowed to whether they may have noticed anyone behaving suspiciously. At the ticket office I received the same answer.

Upon contacting the taxi centre in Oslo, I was informed that none of the cars had made any trip out in that timeframe, nor had any hire cars made a journey that could be considered relevant. I also checked all stops on local train lines in the city's surrounding areas, including, of course, the local stop near the scene.

However, I did receive an important piece of information from bus driver **Sigurd Monsen**, who had driven the route into Oslo that same evening. At 6:35 p.m. precisely – he noted the time because he keeps to a strict schedule and would have remembered any deviation – he stopped at a bus stop about 400 metres from Hasselbakken, located on the opposite side of the main road. From the villa, one can reach this stop unseen by walking through the woods, a journey that takes four to five minutes. There, the bus was flagged down by a woman. I include his statement:

'**Monsen, Sigurd**, bus driver, personal details etc., reminded of his legal responsibility etc., states:

I drove the route that day and arrived at the stop near Hestehagen at precisely 6:35 p.m. A woman there waved me down to stop. She boarded and paid her fare to Oslo, where she got off at Tordenskjold's Square. She said nothing during the ride, and I didn't pay much attention to her. There were only three passengers; I knew the others, as they travel with me often, but the woman was unknown to me. As far as I can remember, she wore a large grey hat – I haven't seen any other lady wearing one like it – but it was raining that day, and you see a lot of strange clothing then. She was quite tall for a woman, dressed in a long blue or black cape which was completely soaked by the rain, and I couldn't see much of her face; it's possible she was also wearing a veil, but I'm not certain. I think she also wore

high rubber boots. She paid with a five–krone note, which she had ready, and I gave her 3.50 in change: three one–krone coins and a 50–øre piece.'
– **Sigurd Monsen (signed)**
Read aloud and approved.

I succeeded in locating the other passengers on the same route. They all confirm the above description, though Mrs K. adds that she distinctly remembers the woman did not carry an umbrella. However, she did have with her a small brown handbag. Mrs K. also noticed that the woman was out of breath, as if she had run to catch the bus.

Respectfully,
Jens Karlsen

Document 7.
(Pencil draft in Superintendent Vang's handwriting)

According to a telephone report, the result of the investigation is as follows:

All fingerprints originate from the house's own residents and match the submitted samples. The lace handkerchief has no stains. The bullets were both fired from the same weapon, namely a revolver of calibre .320. The footprint from the women's shoe corresponds to a size 40; the sole is significantly worn, especially on the right side. The imprint is very clear and characteristic, and could possibly become important – perhaps decisive – evidence should suspicion fall on a specific person. Mrs Krebs wears size 37 shoes, her maid size 38; thus confusion here is ruled out.

CHAPTER XII

Document 8
Public Notice:
In connection with the murder of Polish national Jan Kurzcpetowski at Villa Hasselbakken on 7 July this year – which took place between 6:00 p.m. and 7:30 p.m. on said date – a woman is sought who that same afternoon boarded a bus to Oslo at Hestehagen in [location missing].

Her description is as follows:

1.75 m tall, presumably blue eyes, somewhat full figure; she was wearing a black or dark blue wide rain cape, a wide–brimmed grey felt hat, and high black rubber boots. She carried a small brown handbag and was, at the time, quite wet, as it was raining and she had no umbrella. She is believed to wear shoe size 40 and to have been in possession of a revolver calibre .320. Information should be given to the police station or the nearest police authority.

This was an excerpt from the police's initial investigation into the case. As previously mentioned, I have not included everything. I have left out items that seemed to me to be of lesser interest, or which I deemed superfluous in light of what I had already recorded.

Superintendent Vang had involved himself extensively in the deaths of Winterstein and Soten, as well as the matter of the icon. He summoned Falk and sought to collaborate with him, holding lengthy conversations. I have Vang to thank for the opportunity to view the documents; he had borrowed them for a short time and was kind enough to hand them over to me one evening when I met him. He had to return them the next morning, so I stayed up all night copying them to complete my notes with this expert material.

Written on the cover in red pencil and forceful handwriting was:

"**Investigation continues —**"

CHAPTER XIII

Nearly two months passed and the gruesome events faded from memory. Everyday life resumed, time smoothed over our worries, and it became strangely quiet after the storm. For a while, the public's attention had circled around us; those implicated in the 'Hasselbakken Drama', as the newspapers called it. All the spotlights were trained on us: the house, the region, and all of us were photographed and described in detail. In the illustrated press, Anne Marie featured as 'the beautiful lady of Hasselbakken'. Now and then, though at increasingly long intervals, it was said the police had discovered a new lead, and interest would flare up again; the waves rose to house height, and the sea foamed. Then it would sink again; the waves grew softer, the wind calmed, the sea settled once more, and everything was as before.

One day Bjelke suddenly telephoned.

'So you're back in the country!' I said, surprised.

'Yes, I'm on holiday; I'm going hunting with Professor Heim, we're leaving tomorrow.'

'And you completed your assignment, delivered the icon?'

'Yes, of course. I've actually brought something for you; I'd like to meet in person. Are you free this evening?'

I was busy, but the prospect of seeing Bjelke again tempted me. 'Well, I'll make it work,' I said quickly.

We agreed to meet at Bjelke's hotel. 'We'll have a little private celebration,' he said.

I followed the cue and dressed in a dinner jacket.

———

I had only known him briefly, but I felt a surge of joy the moment I saw him again. It was as if something bound us together; I hadn't previously realised how sympathetic I found the man. It wasn't like me to be so spontaneous, but I immediately had to tell him how much I'd appreciated his call and how glad I was to meet him again.

Bjelke rang for two dry martinis to be sent up to the room.

'I bring you greetings from the Blue Madonna,' he said once the cocktails were served.

'She is well pleased. She now rests in a lovely crypt in Częstochowa, in the monastery church on the holy Jasna Góra, where all of Poland makes pilgrimage. This order is technically Roman Catholic, but they agreed to keep the icon for now on behalf of their affiliated Greek Catholic organisation, which lives in exile. And so the two icons are reunited for the first time since 1382! I also have a special greeting for you …'

I may have looked somewhat surprised; he was visibly pleased with something.

'Close your eyes,' he said, rising.

When I opened them again, Madonna's face shone before me. I could tell at once it wasn't the original – it was a coloured lithograph – but it was well-rendered and very vivid.

'A well-known Polish artist made it,' said Bjelke. 'He worked day and night, and in between, he knelt in prayer. That's the kind of man he is. We Norwegians struggle to understand such religious ecstasy.'

He shrugged. 'It's yours.'

'Mine?' I stood, overwhelmed by the gesture.

He smiled. 'It's rather good, isn't it? A nice keepsake.'

'Heaven knows it is,' I said gladly. 'But why give it to me? Surely someone else is closer to it, Krebs, for example?'

Bjelke shrugged dismissively. 'Seriously … Krebs …' was all he said, smiled a little, and continued: 'I had three copies made of the twenty-five produced. I kept one, and this is for you.'

'And the third?'

'I've sent that to Miss Eva Mendel as a memento of her father.'

By now I had gathered myself enough to speak, but I was deeply moved as I said:

'Mr Bjelke, I hardly know you. I don't understand this, and all I can say is I can't imagine a dearer gift …'

Bjelke waved it off. 'That's fine. I'm glad,' he said briefly. 'For heaven's sake, don't tell me you haven't had dinner?'

We found a quiet corner in the hotel's dining room; it was still early in the evening and not busy.

'We'll take it easy,' Bjelke suggested. 'As I said, we'll have a little private celebration, just the two of us. It's been a long time since I was here – apart from this summer, when I was always busy – it's been a full seven years. I came straight from a high–mountain hotel – I was on a whirlwind journey – yes, by God, just passing through …'

'Right then!' The waiter arrived. We ordered – 'A splendid dinner for men,' said Bjelke, immediately snapping out of his reverie. We began with a large spread, open sandwiches, and vintage Lysholmer beer.

'I've been told that you're something of a gourmet,' said Bjelke, 'so you'll understand that I've done my homework.'

Soft music drifted over to us; there are certain moments filled with exuberant well–being, where the tension rises to the surface like pearls in dry champagne. I knew there would be revelations this evening; I felt it in the air.

'I belong, in a way, to the circle around the Madonna too,' I said. 'The others are dead.'

'Shall I pass you the caviar?' he asked.

'No thank you,' I replied.

His light eyes were fixed on me with an attentive expression. 'Yes, the others are dead. But tell me, have you ever formed an opinion on how Winterstein and Soten died?' He looked at me with curiosity.

'I haven't really come to any conclusion,' I said, 'but I must admit I've considered the possibility that …'

'Yes? That …?'

'… that the icon was connected to their deaths, not just psychologically, but in reality.'

'Excellent,' he said, helping himself to caviar. 'Go on.'

'But I had to abandon the theory,' I said dejectedly, 'I couldn't find the connection.'

'Let's have a drink,' he said. 'Cheers! So you found no solution?'

'No. For a while I even entertained the thought that it might be a kind of divine revenge against the desecrators; something akin to the vengeance the old Pharaohs supposedly arranged as protection against grave robbers. I've always had a feeling that there was something mysterious about Lord Carnarvon's famous excavation of Tutankhamun's tomb; he and his companions died one after the other. It's a fact that splendid amulets shaped like sacred scarabs were often placed on the mummies' chests; some of them had pins. Could it be those, or the air inside poisoned over time, or generations of trapped insects, or all of it combined? I've often speculated about it.'

The waiter interrupted us, clearing the first course and bringing the next, sole with hollandaise.

'What shall we drink with this?' asked Bjelke.

'A Rhine wine or perhaps a Mosel. Do you have Berncasteler Doctor on the list?'

'Let me choose,' I said. 'I remember a wine I drank in Cologne the day all this began – the thing that led to us sitting here today – it was called Brauneberger Juffer.'

We ordered a bottle.

'The Borgias also used to protect their secret rooms with poisoned needles,' I returned to the topic at hand. 'Anyone who didn't know the mechanism would prick themselves and die. I've thought of this too, but had to abandon the idea.'

'May I ask why?'

'Because I saw Falk open and close the panel with my own eyes; nothing happened. And Winterstein had the icon in his possession for years. It wasn't that simple.'

'No,' said Bjelke, 'it's not that simple. By the way, this Brauneberger Maiden from the Mosel is delightful.'

We emptied our glasses; the golden wine flowed into our blood and through our hearts, and made it easy to exist. The lighting was soft and subdued. More people had come into the dining room.

'The things you mentioned just now make up an incredibly interesting, though little–known chapter,' said Bjelke. 'There's no doubt that people in earlier times knew of poisons that have long since been forgotten. Jeanne d'Albret, the mother of Henry IV, was, according to reports, poisoned with a pair of gloves. The King of France attempted to murder his enemy, Admiral Coligny, with a book he sent as a gift; its pages were laced with poison. If the recipient moistened his finger when turning the pages, it was over for him; that was how refined the method was.

'And Philip of Milan killed his wife by applying violet poison to her lips, expecting her lover would kiss her; that was the Renaissance in all its wild majesty. With Marie de' Medici and her court poisoner, Maître René, France faithfully followed. The poisoners grew famous, and it became fashionable to keep poisons and antidotes in one's medicine cabinet. Spouses removed one another; heirs helped speed up inheritances, and to deal with the problem, Louis XIV even established a special court solely for such cases: the Chambre Ardente, as you may recall. Am I boring you?'

'No, on the contrary.'

'One of the most fascinating cases was without a doubt the Marquise de Brinvilliers, who poisoned her father and her two brothers. When she then began poisoning her husband, her lover gave him an antidote, and the poor man hovered for months between life and death, but eventually died. Her lover, Sainte–Croix, had his own laboratory where he conducted his experiments, wearing a glass mask over his face. But one day something went wrong; he dropped the mask and collapsed as if struck by lightning. The state seized his laboratory and handed it over to France's scholars. But note this: it turned out Sainte–Croix had been far more advanced than them.

'The doctors were completely baffled by the poisons they found. They could not be detected either by analysis or in their effects. They tested them on animals, which died after a short or long period depending on the poison, but no trace could be found in their organs; they appeared healthy and normal. Especially mysterious was a white powder. It may have been the last time the Borgias' famous secret snow–white poison – the so–called 'succession powder' – was used! Modern doctors often claim it was just arsenic, but I point out in response that arsenic was already well–known back then. Incidentally, only a few years ago, a South African laboratory discovered a new poison called Adenis, which is five thousand times more deadly than strychnine. So it's possible that toxicology still holds its undiscovered secrets.

'Professor Heim agrees with me. The famous poisoners naturally had great insight and vast practical experience – it was, after all, their livelihood. They of course wrote down their recipes, and had students to whom they bequeathed their secrets. If such a book were to suddenly come to light and be exploited without conscience, it's likely that modern science would have many riddles to solve.'

'It's essentially the old problem of the arms race between cannon and armour,' I said. 'When the cannon becomes more effective, armour catches up. New inventions appear, and defence gains the upper hand, until the cannon takes the lead again. They spur each other on. But in toxicology, offensive means have, of course, not developed over the last few centuries – no great poisoners have emerged, the attack has stagnated, and so has defence, because it's had no stimulus. But why are we talking about all this? The sole was quite good, wasn't it?'

Bjelke nodded. 'I'm enjoying an evening like this. My life is otherwise quite unpredictable. One can live dangerously these days, and also make a good living from it, though it doesn't always turn out as comfortably as tonight.'

He was about to continue, but the waiter arrived just then. The next course was tournedos with a bottle of Chambertin. The wine glowed ruby red in the glasses. Our conversation flowed easily and naturally about everyday matters but our chat wasn't frivolous in the slightest.

'Now it's your turn,' I said. 'You once said that everything was perfectly clear to you. If I remember correctly, you even used the expression that the evidence was obvious.'

Bjelke looked at me curiously. 'What is it you want to know?'

'You asked me about Winterstein's and Soten's deaths. I answered. Now I'm waiting for you.'

'Alright,' said Bjelke. 'It all began when Jan returned to Europe. All those years, the events in Olesko gnawed at him. Strangely enough, he blamed himself; deep down, he was a religious soul, and his goal was to become a monk again. He had grown up in the monastery, and of course that had shaped him. Circumstances had thrown him out into the world, and at times he felt deep remorse over what he had taken part in as a soldier. He travelled to

Częstochowa, where representatives of the Greek Catholic Pauline Order had taken refuge with their Roman Catholic counterpart. He told his story, but was met with suspicion. Among other things, they asked him why he hadn't come earlier.

'I don't know if you recall a trial in Piotrków in 1912, when it came to light that monks had looted the famous Black Madonna of jewels worth a fantastic sum. At that time, the Madonna's diamond–encrusted crown was valued at no less than eighteen million marks. Some of the stones had been stolen and replaced with fakes. Anyway, it ended with one of the monks, Damazy Macoch, being sentenced to fifteen years of hard labour for murder, theft, forgery, and moral crimes. It was a bombshell, and that mistrust still lingers among the top leadership today.

'But somehow Jan managed to come to an agreement with the order; on the condition that he returned the Madonna icon, he would be granted absolution for all the years he had wandered the world, and would be reaccepted into the order. He then travelled to Germany to begin his investigation. I know he took the matter seriously. First, he established which army units had been stationed in Podolia in December 1918, and then researched the history of those regiments. He then advertised in German newspapers and used the radio's "Where–Are–You–Comrade?" series. His tone grew more and more threatening, and finally, he got a response.

'Soten contacted him first. He had also recently returned to Germany. Soten felt betrayed and cheated by Winterstein, understandably. Soten had also been relatively passive in Olesko. He and Jan made what seemed like a truce, but there was never any real friendship between them. Their motives were too different. Soten wanted money, his share of the jewels, and the icon's value; Jan wanted the icon above all, to redeem himself. Shall we have a cigarette in the meantime?'

He offered me one and lit it.

'But you?' I asked, 'how did you get involved in all this?'

'Wait a bit. Jan and Soten made an agreement that Soten should act as the leader of the meeting and appear to be the one who had called it. Jan was to arrive unexpectedly. And so the game began: Winterstein on one side, and Jan and Soten on the other. Winterstein lived under a false name for fear of retribution. He had the icon in his possession, but had sold the jewels for forty thousand marks, of which he had given Krebs around ten thousand. Jan and Soten demanded the icon and forty thousand marks, no more, no less. Winterstein claimed they had no legal right to it. He pointed out how slim their chances were if they pursued legal action, and excused himself by saying the forty thousand marks had been lost during the inflation. But he finally offered to raise twenty thousand marks on the condition that they let him keep the icon and waived any claim to it.

'Soten was furious and increased his demands; he insisted, among other things, that Miss Mendel be given ten thousand marks. In short, it became completely impossible to reach an agreement. And when you left the restaurant, the incident with the disguised S.A. men occurred; Winterstein had taken all precautions to stay hidden. Whether the attack was meant solely to delay you, or if the shot that went into the ceiling was intended seriously, I don't know.

'But as you know, Soten still managed to track Winterstein, who then took the icon with him to Norway. By tailing you, he discovered where Krebs lived and expected to find an ally in him, also believing that circumstances in your country would be simpler and more transparent. He had a plan: he wanted the others to incriminate themselves … And he assumed it would be easier to keep an eye on his foreign opponents in Norway than when they were lost in the crowd in their own country.'

'But you …' I said again.

'When Jan notified the Greek Catholic Pauline Order that he had located the icon and that it was in Norway, I was brought into the picture via an international organisation. I was Norwegian and a lawyer, so I could help them with the matter. In the meantime, the first act was played out at Hasselbakken. Winterstein's only aim was to secure a strong position in the coming showdown, which he knew was inevitable. He installed an alarm system and a hidden camera to obtain evidence against his opponents; he assumed they would try to simply steal the icon. At the same time, he arranged through Falk that they be followed from the start, and that a strong net was cast around them. Had they stolen the Madonna that night, they would not have gotten far; he would have had them arrested on the spot and would have had a tactically excellent position in the dispute.'

'But they didn't take the icon with them.'

'No, but he had the photograph of Jan, almost as good. It could be used against him at any moment. Winterstein quite rightly assumed that they wouldn't risk a long and costly lawsuit on such a shaky basis as war spoils; he intended to blackmail them into peace. And the next day, he and Falk went into town and made their demands with the photograph in hand. He offered them twenty–five thousand marks and the photographs, otherwise, he'd report them to the police and take it to court. Soten was furious, and it nearly came to blows, but Jan was frightened and persuaded him to accept a settlement. While waiting for the money, they agreed to stay at Hasselbakken; mutual distrust dictated this step.'

'So that's why they suddenly became friends,' I said.

'Seemingly,' said Bjelke. 'Winterstein was already lost. Despite his cunning, he had been outsmarted.'

He was interrupted by the waiter – that damn waiter – we sent him away, cancelled the rest of the meal, and asked for coffee with Armagnac. We were silent for a while, lost in our thoughts. There was a low murmur of voices in the dining room, but everything was muffled by thick carpets; even the voices became subdued and intimate.

'You said he had been outsmarted—' I repeated.

Bjelke looked at me attentively. 'That was Winterstein's great mistake,' he said. 'Winterstein had convinced himself that Jan and Soten wanted to steal the icon. That may well have been true in Soten's case, but Jan deceived them both. That's how Winterstein's death became inevitable, precisely when he thought he held the trump card. The arrow was already nocked, and the bow was drawn …'

He paused. 'Did you also think Jan came that night just to steal the icon?' he asked.

'No,' I said, confused. 'I remember wondering why the two of them were so easily scared off.'

'I believe they had a raging quarrel that night,' said Bjelke, laughing softly. 'They got into the room without trouble; no one was home to watch, everything was suspiciously well–arranged. And then, the usually cold–blooded Jan was suddenly seized by a strange fear and wanted to leave. He fled, dragging the furious Soten with him. Of course, it was an act, because Jan had already done what he came to do. He had achieved his goal.'

'Goal?'

'Here,' Bjelke pulled some photographs from his wallet; I had seen them before. They were the photos of Jan on the night of the break–in. 'Look at these; can you see him doing anything with the panel?'

'He's trying to open it?'

'No, his hand is higher, at least ten centimetres above the dove's head. He's standing there calmly, but then hears the camera whirring and turns around. But by then he had already done what he came for.'

'And that was?'

'When you turn the dove's head to the right to open the panel, it triggers a spring, and a fine needle snaps out and strikes the right thumb. The needle is coated with an instantly lethal poison! That's the Madonna's secret. That's where the legends of the Madonna's vengeance come from.'

'But I've opened the panel myself, and Falk too,' I said, incredulous.

'You know, of course, the holy numbers and their symbolic significance,' said Bjelke.

'The panel was externally decorated with the Trinity, and the needle only triggers every third time the icon is opened. Be sure – Jan timed it precisely.'

The solution still struck me as too ridiculous; I was still sceptical.

'But Winterstein had the icon all those years; he should have been killed long ago,' I said. 'I'm sure he looked at it every day.'

'Winterstein didn't know the secret,' said Bjelke. 'The needle was secured the whole time the Madonna was in his possession, do you understand? Jan's task on the night of the break-in was to remove the safety and set the Madonna of Vengeance in motion. I assume the prior in Borodjanka, when he sent Jan off with the icon, had told him the secret and shown him how to disable the safety mechanism if necessary. Jan didn't have time for that back in Olesko, but it was in his thoughts; it was his last word on the doorstep. The needle only works when the safety is disabled; it's like a pistol. Twice, the panel can be closed without anything happening; each time the spring is wound a little. But the third time, when the panel is opened, it strikes fatally!'

'Strange,' I said. 'So that was it, that simple.'

'In reality, Jan was the one holding the cards,' continued Bjelke. 'All he needed was ten seconds in front of the icon to remove the safety, and then he knew fate would take its course. Winterstein's estate – that is, his devout old sister – could easily be persuaded to give up the Madonna to a religious organisation. Which, incidentally, she has done. As soon as Winterstein was dead, Jan sent a telegram to the order, and they found me the right man to carry on the mission up here.'

'Three times …' I repeated. 'Winterstein showed us the icon on the night of the break–in and closed it; that's once! He must have looked at it the next morning and closed it again; that's twice. And when he came home late that night, he opened it for the third and last time. It fits. Let's see if it also fits with Soten's death,' I continued aloud, thinking. 'When we found Winterstein, the panel was open. Someone closed it; that was the first time, so the spring was half–loaded … The second time was when we all went up to look at the icon, then I closed it and set the needle to full tension … We all contributed to it, and then Soten opened it during the night … So Soten didn't know the secret?' I said. 'By the way, I noticed you were shocked when you heard of his death.'

'I assume Soten gradually became a nuisance,' Bjelke replied, 'and that Jan realised it was his intention to act on his own. Soten's motive was money, pure and simple, and the Madonna was worth millions, remember that. That's why Jan, as a precaution, left the needle unsecured. It's quite clear that Soten died during an attempt to steal the icon. He had arranged for sleeping draughts in the others' drinks, to ensure he had a free hand. Soten was an unusually strong man and just barely managed to return to his own room. Winterstein collapsed on the spot.'

'But how do you know all this?' I asked, looking at him inquisitively. 'Have the Pauline Order initiated you into the secret as well?'

'Me? Are you mad? I, a non–believer; no, dear friend. But the evidence was practically in my hands from the very first evening. It was immediately clear to me that the deaths had to be intimately connected to the icon in one way or another, since the panel was always left open. Then I received photographs of Jan's and Soten's fingerprints, and I studied them both. But the right thumb showed no sign of any cut! That confused me, and my theory collapsed like a house of cards. Then it was the matchbox holder that solved the problem for me. Do you remember the matchbox that stood in Soten's room? Shall we order another glass of Armagnac? It was excellent.'

He signalled to the waiter.

'I can't understand what the matchbox could have told you,' I said impatiently.

'No?' he said, smiling with irritation. 'Well, it had been struck once on the left side – otherwise, it was new. So Soten was left–handed! Do you see now how important that discovery was?'

'By God,' I exclaimed, 'you're absolutely right; Winterstein said that Soten fired with his left hand in Daudsewas.'

'So I naturally had to look at the left index finger to find the cut. And there it was.

'And when I then received the icon, I carried out a test using a long pair of tongs, which I wrapped with plasticine roughly to the thickness of a thumb so that the needle wouldn't break. It all matched perfectly – but it is quite the devilish contraption.'

The waiter came over and interrupted him.

'So that was how Winterstein and Soten died,' I murmured. 'But couldn't an autopsy have revealed all this?'

Bjelke looked at me.

'I thought you knew. Vang took a keen interest in the two previous deaths, and he arranged for Soten's body to be examined, but they found nothing. There are more poisons between heaven and earth than are dreamt of in a pharmacopoeia from 1935,' he added mockingly.

'But you understood the connection and you said nothing …'

'It wasn't my business. My task was to retrieve the icon. Besides—' he gave me a sudden hard glare, '—do you think Vang would cooperate with me, an outcast? Am I to be expected to wait in the antechamber to assist anyone?'

There I had him in a flash. Beneath the surface, he was bitter and raw about the past. He felt redundant in a field where he had once been indispensable, and he suffered for it. Such was his attitude, this man who, by all accounts, had ruined his own chances, gambled recklessly with his fate, and lost everything save the opportunity and the right to live dangerously. I sat observing him. Suddenly, I saw him flinch; his mouth drew into a tight, tormented line, and his eyes shone with a terrible intensity. Music had begun to play.

'Do you know the melody?' I asked, trying to distract him.

He did not respond. I repeated my question.

'It is Pergolesi's: *Tre giorni son che Nina* …' he whispered at last, his teeth clenched, his face contorted.

'What's come over you?' I asked, surprised.

CHAPTER XIV

It lasted only a moment. He quickly gathered his wits; perhaps the music had stirred some memories within him …

I felt completely at ease; a slight thrill tingled within me. I was fresh and free and full of energy, and I lived with every cell and nerve. The light Egyptian tobacco, the fragrant night–black mocha, the aroma of sun–drenched Armagnac, all of it lay over me like a blessed veil. All the while I saw Bjelke's intense, attentive face; the world outside our table no longer existed.

Suddenly I heard him say, casually, indifferently:

'How are our friends at Hasselbakken, by the way; are they still married?'

It flashed through my head like a lightning–swift danger signal. I felt confused, caught off guard.

'Yes, they are,' I said. 'But what do you mean by that?'

He didn't answer immediately.

So I continued. I felt compelled to say it:

'You naturally have a theory about Jan's death as well?'

He looked at me for a moment, then nodded.

'Yes, but my theory is quite different from the one Vang and Falk were working with; they've probably given up the whole case by now.'

'What are you referring to?' I asked calmly.

'Well, you know Falk,' he said. 'Falk with his unshakeable conviction that the key to any case lies in its psychological premise. He always tries to "psychoanalyse" his way to a result, and sometimes he succeeds, sometimes he doesn't. Psychology and technique are his two hobbyhorses; he's a method man through and through, and sometimes he gets Vang to follow his lead.'

'And what view is that?'

'That none of the people involved in the case were capable of committing murder. Therefore, the murderer must be outside this circle. They've considered all possibilities; they've made telegraphic inquiries about Miss Mendel, as you probably know, and they seriously believe in some unknown episode in Jan's past life. They've even entertained the idea that his order might have wanted to get rid of him.'

'And you – have you no … method?' I asked, lightly.

'No,' he replied, 'at least no theories that lock me in, I hope.'

It had grown warm in the room; we had drunk heavily, and I suddenly felt like an ice–cold highball. While we waited for it, I remember we passed the time discussing its qualities. We concluded it was to the mind what the final plunge in the steam bath is to the body. In this way, we chatted idly for a long while. We both knew we had drunk quite a bit, but we weren't tipsy.

'To return to the matter at hand,' I said at last, 'surely you can't deny that psychology plays a key role in murder cases.'

Bjelke shook his head. 'In some cases, yes,' he answered. 'In others, it is pure and simple chance that tempts a man to take a life. I don't believe you can, in advance, single out a group of people and say that such and such are capable of murder, while the rest are above suspicion. Fate, environment, and circumstance can often transform a man. I know personally that certain things can happen; on a few occasions I've unfortunately found myself in situations where I had no choice but to take a human life. But that doesn't automatically make me a member of some exclusive murderers' guild. We are all capable of killing when we must!

'I have a friend who fought in the war. Once, he shot a German with his revolver in a trench. And the sight haunts him to this day. He abhors hunting, he cannot bring himself to kill even a fly, and he raises his children to never harm a living creature. But the same man once "bombed" an entire Arab tribe as a pilot in Palestine; he blew them to pieces, as they had been on their way to attack a colony. And that scene never haunts him; he had to act. All that said, he is one of the bravest men I know,' he concluded, unprompted.

Our conversation had drifted somewhat. I offered him a cigarette, and the music changed to the Barcarolle from *The Tales of Hoffmann*. We listened to it for a while.

'My theory about Jan's death is quite different,' he said suddenly. 'Would you like to hear it?'

He looked at me intently; there was a peculiar expression in his eyes.

'Gladly.'

'There are only five people to consider,' he said. 'Krebs and his wife, Falk, and then you and I. One of us killed Jan; I could almost say it doesn't matter which of us.' 'But all of them have solid alibis,' I said, tense. 'I've read the documents.'

I had forgotten my cigarette and had to light it again.

'Solid?' he repeated indifferently. 'What does that mean, since we're dealing with a perfect alibi?'

It was my turn to repeat: '—the perfect alibi …'

My heart suddenly began to pound and tighten. I knew what was coming.

Bjelke's voice was cool and impersonal as he continued:

'Everything suggests that Jan knew the person who came at six o'clock that day. He merely put down the newspaper, and expected no attack. He was a cautious man, and carried his loaded pistol in his inside pocket, but he had no time to draw it. Perhaps he assumed the other person wasn't dangerous.'

'You don't just draw a pistol because a lady comes to visit,' I said.

Bjelke gave a cold smile and sat silent for a moment. 'You've seen the report of the various alibis?' he finally asked.

I nodded.

'And nothing in it strikes you?'

When I didn't answer, he continued:

'Krebs is out of the equation; he really was playing at the time in question and his wife was occupied, both of them with ordinary tasks. So was Falk; he was working in his office. There's only one alibi that bears the mark of having been deliberately constructed …'

'Well then—' I said calmly, I knew what was coming; the game had to be played to the end. 'Well?'

'It's your alibi,' he said. 'Because you deliberately "forgot" your season ticket.'

'This has turned into quite an interesting evening,' I remarked indifferently. 'It started well; it's a pity it must end like this.'

Bjelke suddenly placed his hand over mine. 'Listen now,' he said, 'we're both men. I've heard you described as an old bachelor, an eccentric, a student–society comedian. But I've long since seen that you're made of different stuff. You yourself asked to hear my theory. You've heard it; that's all. I've told you more about myself this evening than I've told anyone else, and I stand entirely outside this matter, so why not take the opportunity to speak openly, man?'

His tone was harsh, almost brutal. I sat for a while staring into my glass. Bubbles rose; bubbles, bubbles …

'Well then,' I said at last. 'I accept your friendship. You shall hear the whole of it.'

Again, I sat for a while without speaking. Time passed, the bubbles burst at the surface, then I pulled myself together.

'You called it a perfect alibi,' I murmured.

'Yes,' he said, 'it's an old trick, an effective one, but curiously, relatively rare: disguising oneself as a woman. I would honestly be very interested to know the details of your alibi. You have, of course, my word of honour regarding discretion.'

'Well,' I said, 'you shall have the details. The whole thing was based on the fact that the train heading into Oslo at 6:00 p.m. stops in a mountain cutting to allow another train to pass before the next station. The train is usually on time; it takes six minutes to reach this cutting. From there to Hasselbakken is a quarter of an hour's walk, if one walks quickly or jogs. From Hasselbakken to the stop for the bus route is four minutes through the woods. That makes twenty–five minutes in total. The bus leaves at 6:35 p.m. So I had ten minutes at my disposal!

'In a locked suitcase – my landlady has never seen its contents – I had some clothes that belonged to my deceased sister. I knew I could make use of one thing or another because she had once lent me some garments back when, as you put it, I once was a comedian in the student society. I packed a hat, a skirt, a loose cape, a pair of high rubber boots, and a pair of women's shoes into a small hand-bag, which I hid in the forest near Hasselbakken. Then I boarded the train and told the conductor I had forgotten my ticket, thus ensuring he would remember me later. I disembarked at the cutting and hid behind a shed until the train had passed, then I ran through the woods until my vision blurred red and I could taste blood in my mouth. I reached the place, changed into the shoes, and went straight in. We exchanged a few words, I shot him down, returned to the forest, put on the skirt, the hat, the cape, and the rubber boots. I couldn't wear the shoes, they pinched too much.

'Yes, and then I took the bus, got off in Oslo and changed in a stairwell; my hat and coat were in the suitcase. I went straight to the café and had a couple of highballs; I genuinely needed them. I asked for illustrated magazines, they swam before my eyes, but I looked through them; I eventually had a whole stack in front of me. That sort of thing sticks in the memory, doesn't it? A waiter may never be able to say precisely how long a guest sat in a café, but a detail like the illustrated magazines, he'll remember that. But I believe I'll need another highball tonight as well,' I added.

'My compliments for not exaggerating anything,' said Bjelke. 'So you left behind a woman's handkerchief, and you deliberately left a footprint from the shoe near the entrance?'

I nodded.

'I suspected it had happened more or less that way,' said Bjelke. 'So the Hasselbakken drama no longer holds any mystery for the two of us. We've exchanged our knowledge this evening. I believe you won't regret having told me this.'

'No,' I said, 'since the person I would most have liked to confide in—'

'I did ask whether the two of them were still married,' said Bjelke, when I didn't continue.

There was a murmur of conversation in the hall, and cigarette smoke drifted low across the tables. I looked at the clock instinctively; it was around midnight.

'But I'll wager you still have one weak point,' he said jokingly. 'That you, after all, have made a blunder.'

The line struck me like a flash of light; I had to smile, as he was quite right. This man knew and understood much – his life had taken such a turn – he had been through things beyond ordinary comprehension. Just a few months earlier, I had walked the broad, safe, ordinary highway – a pedestrian of everyday life like everyone else – but that was long ago now. In the future, I too would understand more; I had eaten from the tree of time, the tree of knowledge of good and evil!

'You're right,' I said. 'I kept the shoes, and the matching handkerchief to the one I left behind. I've even been so careless as to have them at home. But the revolver – I threw that away.'

We both had to smile.

'It's a bit more distant now,' I said. 'But for a time I brooded night and day over why it had to happen, and I searched for a connection. I went over all the things that had happened, everything I had heard about that furious, wild ride from Olesko. At times, lying sleepless and pondering, I told myself that it hadn't happened at all, or at least that it had no meaning. Those three riders came; they were shadows, reflections on the water's surface. I threw a stone, and the ripples spread. A little while later, the surface lies calm again as if nothing has happened.

'I think I now understand why everything went the way it did. They came, those mercenaries from a wild and desperate time, and we couldn't defend ourselves against them. The time itself was in their favour; the newspapers we opened every day spoke of war, violence, blood, and iron. They carried with them an atmosphere of will and action, yes; why not say it outright? Of crime! Of contempt for human life! Let me share one small detail. Winterstein mentioned a clash at a front station in Podolia, and of how Soten had killed a couple of people …

'*But Soten didn't remember it!* It wasn't an act on his part; it had simply slipped from his memory. In that environment, I too was altered; in a wolf pack, one must become a wolf oneself, right? But I gave him a chance. I demanded an immediate promise to leave and never come back. He laughed scornfully – and I shot him. He held me in such contempt that it never even occurred to him to reach for his pistol.'

'I thought as much,' muttered Bjelke, more to himself than to me, 'I suspected something of the sort. But why did you kill him just then; what triggered it?'

'For God's sake, man,' I said, 'I was sitting on my veranda on that last summer's day, watching the two of them through my binoculars. And I saw him kiss her down there on the slope! And she let him! Then I knew my time had come. I've been waiting, man – waiting a thousand days and a thousand and one nights – for her. One day I knew she would walk away, and that from that moment she would belong to me. But then these men came … And I couldn't count on Adrian …'

My ears roared, my eyes swam, the room was wrapped in a fog – I saw only Bjelke's light eyes – and I went on in a kind of ecstasy, swept away by memories, anticipation, hope:

'One day I will reveal myself. One day I'll stand before her and I'll have my proof with me: a pair of worn shoes and a handkerchief, for otherwise she won't believe me … One day, when she is weary and disappointed, and the weight of daily life presses hopelessly upon her … And I will say: Look at me – I have killed!'

'I thought as much,' muttered Bjelke, more to himself than to me, 'I suspected something of the sort. But why did you kill him just then; what triggered it?'

'For God's sake, man,' I said, 'I was sitting on my veranda on that last summer's day, watching the two of them through my binoculars. And I saw him kiss her down there on the slope! And she let him! Then I knew my time had come. I've been waiting, man – waiting a thousand days and a thousand and one nights – for her. One day I knew she would walk away, and that from that moment she would belong to me. But then these men came … And I couldn't count on Adrian …'

My ears roared, my eyes swam, the room was wrapped in a fog – I saw only Bjelke's light eyes – and I went on in a kind of ecstasy, swept away by memories, anticipation, hope:

'One day I will reveal myself. One day I'll stand before her and I'll have my proof with me: a pair of worn shoes and a handkerchief, for otherwise she won't believe me … One day, when she is weary and disappointed, and the weight of daily life presses hopelessly upon her … And I will say: Look at me – I have killed!'